PERSPECTIVES ON GULLIVER'S TRAVELS

PERSPECTIVES ON GULLIVER'S TRAVELS

K.M. JAN
SHABNAM FIRDAUS

Published by
ATLANTIC PUBLISHERS AND DISTRIBUTORS
B-2, Vishal Enclave, Opp. Rajouri Garden, New Delhi-110027
Phones : 25413460, 25429987, 25466842

Sales Office
7/22, Ansari Road, Darya Ganj, New Delhi-110002
Phones : 23273880, 23275880, 23280451
Fax : 91-11-23285873
web : www.atlanticbooks.com
e-mail : info@atlanticbooks.com

ISBN 81-269-0345-7

Printed in India at
Nice Printing Press, Delhi

Preface

The book, *Perspectives on Gulliver's Travels* has been written to meet the needs of the students of English Literature at the Honours and the Post Graduate level. It discusses all the significant aspects of *Gulliver's Travels*—the life and works of the author, Jonathan Swift, the philosophical background, the satire, irony, structure, prose style, misanthropy, misogyny, the chapter-wise summary of the book with critical comments. Besides, the book will be of interest to all those who are interested in Jonathan Swift as a satirist, as it embraces the entire spectrum of the various aspects of the rich and complex satiric *magnum opus* of Jonathan Swift.

The chapter-wise summarisation of the book with critical comments was done by Miss Shabnam Firdaus and the discussion of the different aspects of *Gulliver's Travels* was undertaken by me. This division of labour has led to the early preparation of the manuscript. I hope the book will be found useful for those who are interested in the understanding and enjoyment of *Gulliver's Travels* in the right perspective.

K.M. JAN

CONTENT

1

The Life of Jonathan Swift

Jonathan Swift (1667-1745) was born of English parents in Dublin in 1667. Unfortunately his father died before his birth and the mother and the son lived on the little financial aid that they received from their relatives. He studied at Kilkenny school and graduated from Trinity college, Dublin. For a number of years, he remained private secretary to the essayist and retired diplomat, Sir William Temple who was his distant relative. William Temple entered into controversy over the superiority of the classics over modern literature. Swift's first important work, *The Battle of Books,* a satire on both the parties was written at this time but not published. In the service of William Temple the pride of Swift was hurt by the fact he, a man of superior intellect, was employed by a man far inferior to him. Thus he spent ten years of his life in Moor Park, Surrey in bitterness. When it became unbearable, he left his job to enter the Church of England as dean. But soon after he had to settle in the little church of Laracor, Ireland. Though he hated to be in Ireland, he was compelled to earn his living there.

Swift was honest in his church duties. He cared for the unhappy people around him. But he was himself unhappy to see people of less merit on high position, while his talent went unnoticed. Sir William Temple was a whig. Swift made frequent visits to London and made friends with important Whig writers including Addison. At Laracor, he wrote *The Tale of a Tub* and published it with the *Battle of Books* in 1704. It brought to light his talent as a satirist. Then he left the church and joined the party politics of his day. It was the age of pamphleteering and he was so excellent a pamphleteer that he had no rival. He annoyed the Whigs for their neglect of him and their favour to dissenters. He joined the Tories in 1710 when Queen Anne ascended the throne and remained an important person in London from 1710 to 1713. He was intimate with the writers in the circle of Queen Anne, Pope, Gay, Prior, Thomas Parnell and Dr. Arbuthnot. Despite his intimacy with important Tory leaders and his position as the leading Tory pamphleteer, he could not secure a more important position in the church than the Dean of St. Patrick Cathedral in Dublin, because Queen Anne was herself suspicious of the writer of *The Tale of Tub,* a satire on the Roman Catholic church, the church of England and the Protestant dissenters. He was a power in Tory politics and founded Scriblerous club whose members were Pope, Arbuthnot, Gay and Harley. The aim of the club was to satirize the abuses in the person of a pedant, Martin Scribler. During this period Swift was feared and honoured but he grew quite arrogant as his personal writings reveal. He sought position of power and influence but it became impossible as the Whigs came to power in 1714 with the accession of George I.

Swift was interested in the position of a bishop in England which he could not secure and he was compelled to spend his days in Ireland. Though he hated to be in wretched Ireland he was moved by the economic plight of the Irish people to write *Drapier's Letters* in 1724. It was at attack on the government proposal for a new Irish coinage. With this he became popular with the Irish people and produced other pamphlets like "Short view of the Present State of Ireland" (1727) and "A Modest Proposal" (1727). The last days of Swift were also spent in Dublin where he wrote his best-known work, *Gulliver's Travels.* He stayed in Dublin with reluctance and a feeling that fate did not smile on a deserving man. His bitterness reached the point of insanity. He silently bore the sorrow of the death of Esther Johnson, a beautiful young woman, the illegitimate daughter of William Temple who loved Swift ever since they met in the house of Temple. *The Journal to Stella* was addressed to this lady. Another woman, Hester Vanhomrigh whom Swift called Vanessa, fell in love with him and followed him to Dublin. It was an embarrassing situation with which Swift dealt with humour and sometimes with anger. The symptoms of a brain disease which had appeared earlier also aggravated his madness. He died in 1745 leaving behind his will to found St. Patrick's Asylum for lunatics and incurables. Today it stands as "a silent monument of strange genius."

2

THE WORKS OF JONATHAN SWIFT

Jonathan Swift was a great satirist. He had an exceptional genius for satire. He disliked shams, pretensions, vanity and injustice and stripped them of the illusory glamour in order to expose their reality through his perfect technique of irony. His genius for satire is reflected in an interesting incident of his early years in London. There was an astrologer, Patridge who made forecasts. Swift made predictions for the year 1708 as determined by the unerring stars in his "Bickerstaff Almanac." His first prediction was related to Patridge, the almanac maker: "I have consulted the star of his nativity by my own rules and find he will infallibly die upon the 29th of March next about eleven at night of a raging fever; therefore I advise him to consider of it and settle his affairs in time." On 30th March the newspaper published a letter with the details of Patridge's death and next day "Elegy of Mr. Patridge" appeared. When Patridge lost his clients, he published the denial of his burial. Swift refuted it through astrological calculations that Patridge was dead in "Vindication of Isaac Bickerstaff."

The incident reflects the satiric style of Swift. He suggests the remedies of hypocrisy and injustice by magnifying the atrocity and defending it with a seriousness that brings the satire to the surface. One such example of this style is found in "Argument to Prove the Abolishing of Christianity May Be Attended with Some Inconveniences," where he points out the needed reforms. As Swift worked as secretary to Sir William Temple who was a Whig and supporter of the Ancients against the Moderns, Swift wrote his "Battle of Books" in support of the Ancients in 1696-98 and published it with "A Tale of a Tub" in 1704. In 1710 he prefixed an "Apology" to A Tale of a

Tub where he explained his motive. *The Battle of Books* contains the quarrel between the spider and the bee which serves to represent the dispute between the ancients and the moderns. The spider states the difference between the two types of intellectuals through these allegorical symbols intended to favour him. But it has the opposite effect:

> "Your livelihood is a universal Plunder upon Nature; a Freebooter over Fields and Gardens and for the sake of stealing will rob a Nettle as readily as a violet whereas I am a domestick Animal, furnished with a Native stock within myself. This large castle to shew my improvements in the Mathematicks is all built with my own Hands and the Materials extracted altogether out of my own Person."

This play of the idea and the image which we find here does not characterise Swift's later works. The bee stands for the ancients who drew upon various corners of nature producing honey and work but the moderns are like the spider who spins out of himself and shares its narrow poisonous outlook. Finally, this matter in his life remained undecided. In the Apology which Swift affixed to "A Tale of Tub" in 1710 he throws light on his motive which was to proceed in a manner that should be altogether new, the world having been already too long nauseated with endless repetitions upon every subject. The abuse in religion, he proposed to set forth in the Allegory of coats and the three brothers, which was to make up the body of the discourse. Those in learning he chose to introduce by way of digression...." "A Tale of Tub" is a satire on the Roman Catholic Church, the church of England and the Protestant dissenters by exposing the fact that all churches, religion, service and statesmanship are nothing but hypocrisy. The allegory of the coat is the best part of the satire. An old man dies and leaves a coat (the Christian truth) to each of his three sons, Peter, Martin and Jack with the elaborate instruction for the care and the use of the coat. It turns out to be a satire on all religious sects as the way the sons, Martin, Peter and Jack change the father's will by changing the fashion of the coat. The device of translating developments into theology and ritual—the parody of the physical accompaniment of a coat to satirize superstition and dissenting fanaticism turns religion into a religious equation with trivial and external trimmings. Swift opposes pride and fanaticism by reason but he was a staunch supporter of the church of England and did not favour tolerant treatment of the dissenters. The satiric device of Swift is here to obliterate the difference and the sign. His "Modest Proposal" (1729) puts forward the idea that the children of Ireland should be raised for the dining table of the rich Englishmen. The motive behind the satire seems to portray the poverty of the Irish people and the indifference of the English politicians to their suffering. The intensity of protest is strongly registered through the mask of complete indifference between animals and children. It is the indictment of the conditions under which these children are forced to live. The quiet and matter-of-fact tone of Swift in which he, like a merchant, persuades his customers of the superior quality of his goods enhances the ironical effect. It is the example of the brilliant irony of Swift which reveals that these children would be better if they are treated like animals than in their present condition.

Jonathan Swift's reputation rests as a writer on *Gulliver's Travels.* It is a children's classics, a tale of adventures like *Robinson Crusoe* and at the same a very intelligent satire on mankind. *Gulliver's Travels,* appears to be a travelogue, an account of the four imaginary voyages of one Lemuel Gulliver to four different countries. Gulliver's first voyage ends in a shipwreck which brings him to Lilliput which is inhabited by people as tall as thumb. Gulliver gives almost a realistic account of the details of his stay with them and their way of living. They were only six inches tall so that when Gulliver came back he put some of them into his pocket. Their houses, plants and animals are accordingly of very small size and the size of the Lilliputians is quite symbolic. It, in fact, reflects the smallness or littleness of humanity. The politicians of Lilliput are engaged in tight-rope dancing and dancing to the rhythms of the movement of the stick in the hand of the king or his minister. Their political and religious parties are engaged in petty quarrels. The two parties, the Little-Endians and the Big-Endians, quarrel over whether an egg should be broken on its little and or big end. The entire country is plunged into a civil war. It is a satire on the contemporary politics of Swift's age. Swift has removed the film of familiarity from the world he describes and presents an interesting adventure story like *Robinson Crusoe.*

Lemuel Gulliver's second voyage brings him to the land of Brobdingnag which is inhabited by the giant size people. It offers a contrast to the land of Lilliput and here everything is carried on a large scale. The inhabitants of Brobdingnag are sixty foot high. Gulliver tells the Brobdingnagian king about the ambitions, wars, victories of his own world. The king wonders that such meanness can exist in such little odious vermin that the earth ever suffered to crawl upon.

The third voyage of Gulliver brings him to the land of Laputa. It is a satire on philosophers and scientists. Laputa is a flying island and the professors at the academy of Lagado are of airy constitution. The way a scientist is engaged for eight years in extracting sunrays from cucumbers is peculiarly Swiftian satire on science and speculative philosophy. There is also the description of struldbruggs who are compelled to live on ever after losing physical strength, hope and desire for life. It comes close to the way Swift spent the last days of his life.

The fourth voyage of Lemuel Gulliver brings him to the country of the Houyhnhnms and the Yahoos. The Houyhnhnms are horses but endowed with superior intelligence. On the other hand, the Yahoos seem to present brutish irrationality. It is the bitterest satire on the pride of man and Swift is considered a misanthrope on the ground of this fourth book. It brings to a logical conclusion the satire that began with Gulliver's voyage to the land of Lilliput. When Gulliver gives an account of British institutions, the Houyhnhmn master regards them as the main result of "gross defect in reason and virtue." Gulliver explains "the many virtues of the excellent quadrupeds placed in opposite view to human corruptions had so far opened my eyes and enlarged my understanding that I began to view the actions and passions of men in a very different light and to think that the honour of my own kind not worth managing." Gulliver's disgust with mankind rises steadily and he accepts the superiority of the Houyhnhnms.

The other works of Swift include *The Journal to Stella* and *Drapier's Letter. The Journal to Stella* is the collection of letters written between 1710 to 1713 to Esther Johnson, a girl to whom he had been attached mysteriously. There is an effusion of a kind which reflects a strange temperament somewhat ailing, at times, playful and tender. Probably the bustle of the public life that preoccupied him raised him above the bitterness which is traceable a little earlier, in *A Tale of a Tub*. It is an interesting commentary on men and events of his time. It also contains purely personal passages of love for Esther Johnson. *Drapier's Letters* (1724) are completely different from the previous work which by its argument influenced the cause of Ireland by preventing the debasement of the Irish coinage. There was a general protest to which the Government had to yield. Swift ever remained proud of leading the public opinion on the occasion.

The poems of Swift are satirical in nature and do not touch the highest level above the doggerel in which he shocked the people by highlighting some ugliness and hypocrisy of the society.

3

THE SOURCES OF *GULLIVER'S TRAVELS*

The interest in the sources of *Gulliver's Travels* was evinced by Orrey, Scott, Mon Mason and others long before 1868 when Monck E.H. Knowles made his discovery in *Notes and Queries* [4th series, 1 (1868, 223)]. He found a passage in Sturmy's *Compleat Mariner* (1669) which appeared verbatim in the description of the storm early in the voyage to Brobdingnag. Knowles's examples led to scholars' hunting of verbal parallels or parallels of incident and narrative. Such an example is Borkowsky's "Quellenzu Swift Gulliver" (1893), *Anglia* 15 (1893), pp. 345-89.

Borkwsky tried to demolish the undeserved reputation of Swift by tracing the sources of *Gulliver's Travels.* He compared the relevant passages of *Gulliver's Travels* with More's *Utopia,* Rabelais, Denis Vairasse d'Alais' *L'Histoire de Severambles* (1677-79), Gabriel de Foigmy's *La Terreaustrate Connue* (1676 and especially Cyrano de Bergerac's *L'Historie Comique de la Lune* (1656).

Several discussions of the sources of *Gulliver's Travels* appeared. Max Poll's "The Sources of Gulliver Travels" appeared in 1904 followed by Pietro Toldo's "Les voyages merveilleux de Cyrano de Bergerac et de Swift leurs rapports avee L'oeuvre de Rabelais" in 1906-07. Toldo dealt with Swift's relation with Rabelais. Cyrano showed many parallels with *The Arabian Nights* especially with the story of Hassan-al-Bassri which includes a visit to the land of giants.

William Alfred Eddy's *Gulliver's Travels: A Critical Study* which appeared in 1913 was the result of his misconception of Swift's intention. Therefore he classed it with imaginary voyages especially found in French literature. His discovery of the parallels between the works of Cyrano and *Gulliver's Travels* was only superficial. Cyrano in his French voyages satirized civilization and Christianity in order to glorify man, natural society and natural religion. What Eddy missed was the fact that Swift used Cyrano and the tradition of philosophic voyage not to extend but only to reverse it. Eddy set aside Anthonys Collins' *Discourse of Freethinking* which is a source for Swift's parody into English. Eddy also set aside Segrais' *L'sle Imaginaire* (1658) on the ground that it includes a republic of dogs. He fails to catch the satiric undertones of the philosophic imaginary voyages as a genre. Eddy finds Cyrano's second romance, *L'Histoire comique du Soleil* adequate precedent for alleged scathing denunciation of mankind in the voyage to the Houyhnhnms. He finds in the voyages to Lilliput and Brobdingnag the traces of Berkley's idea of the relativity of human life and its values which he finds in George Berkeley's *A New Theory of Vision* (1709). A.W. Secord finds fault with Eddy in neglecting native sources and traditions especially authentic voyages. Secord's view was then confirmed by the studies of R.W. Frantz and Willard Bonner. Frantz in "Swift's Yahoos and the Voyagers" in 1931 finds the disagreeable traits of the Yahoos to accounts of monkeys and savages in books of authentic travel by Dampier, Herbert and others.

In *Captain William Dampier: Buccaneer-Author* (1934), Willard Bonner finds obvious influence of Dampier in Swift's use of irreverent factual style and his creation of characters like Bickerstaff, Drapier and Gulliver and his practice which varies between imitation and parody. Swift adopts Dampier's authentic style of a plain, serious and honest seaman with his eager curiosity. But the most probable source of the fourth voyage in *Gulliver's Travels* seems to Gelli's *Circe* which was translated into English by Tom Brown in 1702 where Ulysses finds in his conversation with a horse who was earlier a man that he does not want to be transformed into the human form because horses fulfil their nature better than man because they are less handicapped by the nature of their lower parts. Probably the idea of the Houyhnhnm came from this book.

The voyage to Laputa supposed to be the weakest of the voyages appeared to have been derived from Swift's originality rather than from any source material until 1937. Marjorie Nicolson and Nora Mohler in *Annals of Science* discovered Swift's use of *The Philosophical Transactions* for all but two of the projects in the Grand Academy. They also find the origin of the flying machine in the science fiction of his time.

K.W. Frantz returned to the sources of *Gulliver's Travels* in 1938 in "Gulliver's Cousin Sympson" with the discovery of *The New Voyage to the East Indies*, 1715. His view is that William Symson, the pretended author of this imaginary travel may have some connection with Gulliver's fictitious cousin in William Sympson.

The interest in the sources of *Gulliver's Travels* has fallen off for the reason that such discussions have already been made and also because of the awareness that such a study of *Gulliver's Travels* might lead the readers to place the book in a perspective which will cloud rather than illuminate Swift's literary satiric motive. Margaret R. Grennan in "Lilliput and Lupercan: Gulliver and the Irish tradition" in *ELH* (1945) finds Swift's debt to the Irish folklore. Though such a discovery of sources has become a literary pastime, it has, at the same time, highlighted its departure from the tradition of the voyage or travel literature and its greater literary value as a satire.

These studies of Swift's sources of *Gulliver Travels* lead us to the conclusion that Swift made an intelligent and artistic use of the facts that he found in the course of his study. He had an independent mind and a fertile imagination to transmute them into the a completely new artistic form which made his name immortal in the history of English Literature.

4

The Criticism of *Gulliver's Travels* Through the Ages

Ever since Jonathan Swift published *Gulliver's Travels* in 1926, the controversy about the book has continued. In his own age, the author of *Gulliver's Travels* was opposed and the subsequent ages were not sympathetic to him. One of the reasons of such a response was encouraged partly on account of the distorted image of the author as well as his book. Sir Walter Scott noted his extraordinary but "perverse genius." "We are compelled to admire the force of his talents, even while thus unworthily employed in exposing the parts of our nature with the art of anatomist dissecting a mangled and half putrid carcase." In *Gulliver's Travels* Swift committed a libel on human nature. To W.M. Thackeray, one of the most influential of the nineteenth century writers on Swift, the moral of the great satire was "horrible, shameful and great as this Dean is, I say we should hate him." His advice to the readers about the fourth voyage of the book is "Don't read this monster gibbering shrieks and gnashing imprecations against mankind tearing down all shreds of modesty, past all sense of manliness and shame; filthy in word, filthy in thought, furious, raging, obscene." Though we hear nothing of the comic which Fielding found in Swift, almost all the critics of the nineteenth century who described him as perverted genius were compelled to grant a lurid creative power in his writing.

In fact, Swift was not furiously hateful towards mankind. The difficulty with the critics lies in understanding Swift who ran counter to the trend of his age and had no faith in the progressive rational perfection of man and entertained no optimism about the perfectibility of man. The eighteenth century critics were opposed to the view of Swift and rejected his misanthropy while the nineteenth century critics regarded Swift as the image of representative Augustan rationality the reaction against which generated the new spirit of romanticism. Jonathan Swift belongs not so much to the eighteenth or nineteenth century as to the twentieth century which significantly saw the myth of human progress and rational perfectibility being exploded during the first and the second world war. Swift, the rebel of his age, has a definite fascination for the twentieth century and was recast in the image of the hero. The point of transition can be traced in John Middleton Murry's biography of Jonathan Swift. Murry accounts for the morbid negativism in Swift by the disappointment of his ambition in life. Psychoanalysts explain his misanthropy and madness in terms of intense emotional frustration which had its origin in sex. But at the same time, Murry regards him as an artist interested in criticism of the manners and politics of his time. He regards him as a comic writer neither gloomy nor savage but as a believer in religion and the original sin.

F.R. Leavis in his article on Jonathan Swift which is largely devoted to the analysis of *A Tale of a Tub* regards Swift as a great writer and recognises a great negative force to project frustration and constriction where the channels of life have been blocked. Psychologists like Norman O. Brown have tried to study the case history of Swift in his works. But it is a new beginning not a complete study. Literary critics know little about psychoanalysis.

The first step towards the understanding of Swift was the discovery of the true biography of Swift. The result of the work of Recardo Quintana, Louis Landa, Irvin Ehrenpries has been negative but still useful. They have shown that the works of Swift are not merely autobiography. The relationship of Swift with Stella which formed the central fact for Middleton Murry's explanation of the satire appears far less abnormal than it did earlier. The madness of Swift, Meuniere's syndrome is explained by medical science as a distressing but not mentally unbalancing factor and that he suffered from arterio sclerosis. He was irritable and neurotic as many of us are. He is accepted as an artist who could marshall his facts through his brilliantly controlled technique. His craftsmanship produced rationally and emotionally effective results. The biographical investigations have brought to light the fact that this man, though quite passionate, continually worked for the practical solutions to the problems of life. He was proud of being a moderate Tory.

In the fable of *A Tale of a Tub* he advocated the case of the church of England. He proposed many things to help the Irish people economically in *The Modest Proposal.* He was on the side of the established institutions and distrusted radical reform contrary to the beliefs of the common reader. *Gulliver's Travel* presents a balanced picture of human nature with vices and virtues of each society in the voyage. His bitter satire was directed against theorists who gave priority to abstract speculation above practical approach to the everyday problems of man. The literary and intellectual range of Jonathan Swift was very wide. He had studied from the classics to the transactions of the Royal Society. He used the details of his studies and they acquired a profound symbolic significance. Marjorie Nicolson and Nora Mohlar have exhibited that even the voyage to Laputa was not a pure fantasy but the result of his intensive study of the new philosophy and "the projects" are not his inventions.

The articles that have appeared prove that there are references to topical transient events and people in his satire and his greatness lies in transmuting the topical and the transient into something timeless and universal. In 1920 Sir Charles Firth recognised the episodes in Lilliput as an allegory of politicians and events in the England of Walpole. It has been amply demonstrated by Sir Lewis Namier that the satirised corrupt world of Walpole is the microcosm of the moral climate of a nation which is dominated by petty-struggle for power and money and ideal principles are replaced by corrupt practices. It is the symbolic significance of the first voyage of *Gulliver's Travels.*

The study of the eighteenth century intellectual climate shows that it was an age of great revolutionary changes in thought. The old concept of man and his nature was being replaced by the essential and natural goodness of human beings. The shadows of Rousseau's ideas that man is primitively good but spoiled by the society were falling. Swift was aware of the views of the Earl of Shaftesbury that man has an innate moral sense and of the optimistic mechanical philosophy of Lord Bolingbroke who was his old friend and patron. The image of the Yahoo as the natural man contradicts the optimistic estimate of the natural man which runs counter to the classical and Christian view of the original sin.

The real change in the attitude to Swift occurred in 1926 when J.B. Moore remarked that Gulliver is not Swift himself in either intellect or disposition. In his view Gulliver is only an individual dramatic character. He represents neither Swift nor every man. Joseph Horrel in 1943 put forward his analysis of *Gulliver Travels* on the consideration of Gulliver as a persona. It was followed by Ricardo Quintana's "Situational Satire in Swift" where he noted that Swift's method is uniformly by way of dramatic satire. He creates a fully realized character and a fully realized world for him to move in...once the situation has been suggested, once its tone, its flavour have been given, it promptly takes command of itself and proceeds to grow and organize by virtue of its own inherent principles. We can now recognise that the view of Brobdingnag's king of men as "most pernicious race of little odious vermin" is not the view of Swift but part of a conversation that presents only one view of mankind. Thus we observe the reality through the eyes and personality of a beholder through his biases. So there are different vices in the book and no one can be identified with Swift because the dramatic essence remains the essential feature of the situation. This is why we cannot identify Gulliver with Swift. Gulliver is also the victim of irony. So there is not only one point of view in each voyage. Such complications have led to the problem of correct interpretation of the fourth voyage. Swift has been a complex writer. The texture of his writing has a deceptive simplicity. If we take Swift on the literal level, we shall miss the essence of Swift as a satirist. So it is naïve to identify Yahoos with men and condemn Swift as a pessimist. Nor can we find the Houyhnhnms to be ideal as presented in *Gulliver's Travels.* Swift is different from the ordinary satirist where things appear in black and white. Swift is like Shakespeare. As there is no single meaning of a Shakespearean tragedy, there is no single meaning of *Gulliver's Travels* because his art is rich and complex. Therefore it will be a mistake to see Swift's vision of man either wholly good or wholly bad. His view of man partakes of both.

The source of the fourth voyage, Gelli's *Circe* was translated by Tom Brown in 1702 where Ulysses finds in his conversation with a horse who was earlier a man that he does not want to be retransformed into the human form because horses fulfil their nature better than man because they are less handicapped by the nature of their lower parts. But the conclusion of Ulysses is that they are inferior to man because they lack right reason. Swift lived in an age when the place of man in nature was beginning to be questioned by modern thinkers. Locke had debated the question and biology had also removed the barrier that existed between man and beast. The eighteenth century philosophers envisaged the perfection of man through their theory of evaluation. Swift repudiates the contemporary thought through the image of the Yahoo suggesting the lower nature to be the very essence of man. Thus Swift went back to the Christian idea of the original sin which shows that the tendency to fall is inherent in human nature. Swift believed that man could rise above his fallen state or nature also when he rejected the definition of man as "animal rationale" and considered it to be "*rationis capax.*" We are able to understand Swift's position better in the twentieth century because we are better placed than the eighteenth and the nineteenth century people.

We have seen the two world wars, the brutality of man as well as the greatness of man in figures like Mahatma Gandhi and Mother Teresa. It is not difficult for us to take the position that man partakes the nature of the brute as well as the angel. Swift's attitude appears to be that the image of the Yahoo represents the essential man and at times he can rise to the higher level as well. Gulliver finds the features of man in the Yahoo while the king of Brobdingnag, the paragon of human nature is able to understand the corruption in England. It is beyond the power of the Houyhnhnm master because he stands outside the human nature. Swift mirrors the complexity of human nature with the possibilities of bad and good both. It is a position not difficult for us to accept.

5

THE PHILOSOPHICAL BACKGROUND OF *GULLIVER'S TRAVELS*

Gulliver's Travels has generated much controversy ever since its publication among the critics and very few critics seem to have settled the controversy for ever. This is so because *Gulliver's Travels* has been studied as a work of art, impersonal and objective in isolation from the ideas of the author, Jonathan Swift, the Dean of St. Patrick's in Belfast. It was Ernest Taveson who undertook to study *Gulliver Travels* in the light of the religious ideas of Swift in his essay "Swift, The Dean as Satirist" in *The University of Toronto Quarterly* XXII (1953). It is now generally accepted that the fourth voyage of *Gulliver's Travels* does embody a wholly pessimistic view of the place of man and the meaning of his existence in the universe.

Miss Kathleen M. Williams in her article, "Gulliver's Voyage to the Houyhnhnms" in *The Journal of English Literary History* XVIII (1951) points out that the fourth voyage of *Gulliver's Travels* is the culmination of Swift's life-long attack on "the pride of man, especially the pride which convinces him that he can live by the light of unaided reason." Man stands apart both from the "naturally virtuous and rational animal" and irrational ones. Tradition has separated Jonathan Swift, the satirist and Jonathan Swift, the Dean. If we read *Gulliver's Travels* in the perspective of Swift's logical views, much of the misunderstanding and confusion about *Gulliver's Travels* can be removed which cropped up during the last one hundred years after the publication of the book. Jonathan Swift believed in the original sin as interpreted by conservative Anglicanism. He asserted that the doctrine of the original sin is the foundation of the whole Christian religion. In his own statement of personal belief in "Further Thoughts on Religion" he wrote:

> "After his eating of the forbidden fruit, the course of nature was changed.... But men degenerate everyday, merely by the folly, the perverseness, the avarice, the tyranny, the pride, the treachery or inhumanity of their own kind."

The fall of man was an actual event which brought about actual hereditary changes. In "Evening Prayer" Swift highlights the need for the divine grace by repeated reference to the original sin and in his sermon "On the Testimony of Conscience" he rejects the idea "that men's natural faculties are his sufficient moral guides." Swift believed in the Thirty Nine Articles that "Original sin...is the fault and corruption of the nature of every man, that naturally is engendered of the offspring of Adam whereby man is very far gone from original righteousness, and is of his own nature inclined to evil, so that the flesh lusteth always contrary to the spirit and therefore every person born into this world, it deserveth God's wrath and damnation. And this infection of nature doth remain, yea in them that are regenerated, whereby the lust of the flesh...which some do expound the wisdom, some sensuality, some the affection, some desire of the flesh is not subject to the law of God. And although there is no condemnation for them that believe and are baptised; yet the apostle doth confess that concupiscence and lust hath itself the nature of sin." The Article implies the existence of free will, man in spite of his rational faculty has a positive tendency to evil, for which the remedy is in the Gospel. It rejects the Pelagian view dominant in Swift's time that human nature is the same as in the beginning, the corruptions are not of the soul but of the society and perfect life is always possible if men do their best.

This view of man accepts that there is something of the Yahoo even in the best. It goes against Pope's "Essay on Man" where man is situated on "the isthmus of a middle state," the Platonic idea of Renaissance humanism which made man as a fit link in the patterned universe. It is against this background that Swift insists on the significance of the fall.

New beliefs appeared in the time of Swift. The Deists relied on reason, "the belief in the potent concept of innate moral sense." Shaftesbury believed man was naturally adapted to live virtuously in the universe, his sense of right and wrong was warped by man-made environment. Pelagianism was its secular version opposed by the Church. In the eighteenth century, there was a rising faith in progress which assumed perfecting of human behaviour in proportion to the increase of knowledge. The emphasis on completeness and self-sufficiency of man must have seemed to Donne as the signs of "an age of pride." Swift's attack on pride in this background is understandable. His Letter to Pope on September 29, 1925 promises that *Gulliver's Travels* is to present the truth about human nature in opposition to illusion. He points out that man is incorrectly described as "animal rationale" but is really "*rationis capax.*" The suggestion is that reason works against tendencies and can succeed only with effort. Swift's "misanthropy is based on the Christian tradition. Human nature with the tendency towards sin is hateful but there are those who through divine mercy rise above the limitations of the race." So "all my love is towards individuals."

The Yahoos are the hypostatization of irrational mild drives towards evil which men inherit. Yahoos "—two of the brutes appeared together upon a mountain" and by degrees degenerated. It parallels with the change of men after the fall in "Further Thoughts" which is striking. Yahoos being not aborigines suggests that the present nature of man with "its concupiscence and lust" does belong to the original creation. The evidence of the depravity of our nature is revealed by the conduct of the Yahoos (Yahoos' love for shining stones is not understandable to the Houyhnhnm master). The rational creatures cannot understand "the son of Adam." On the contrary, the patriot king of Brobdingnag, despite exemplary virtue understands English behaviour perfectly.

Houyhnhnms have two principal virtues, friendship and benevolence for the whole species. Friendship and benevolence were the favourite words with Shaftesbury and his school who showed that if men followed their real nature, they will have these qualities. Swift wrote in "Consideration upon two Bills," "There are no qualities more incident to the frailty and corruption of human kind than an indifference, or insensibility for other men's suffering." The irony of *Gulliver's Travels* arises from this fact also that friendship and benevolence are part of the essential nature of other species than human beings. Men act in this way only with the grace of God. The irony also consists in the contrast of Gulliver's grief for the master at the time of departure with the cool benevolence of the latter: "When all was ready, and the day came for my departure, I took leave of my master and lady and the whole family, my eyes flowing with tears, and my heart sunk with grief. But his Honour, out of curiosity and perhaps (if I may speak it without vanity) partly out of kindness, was determined to see me in my canoe, and got several of his neighbouring friends to accompany him."

To regard Swift just as a classical moralist with only a tinge of Christianity goes against the whole tenor of his work. He believed that an ideal life was not possible without the knowledge which the revelation provides. Christianity assumes that it is the divine love and compassion which makes possible the redemption of man. This redemption produces a moral grandeur which is not possible for the purely rational to achieve. Gulliver is attacked by savages on the sea and rescued by the European sailors. It suggests the rejection of the idea of the primitive virtue. Overemphasis on the misanthrophy has eclipsed the relative goodness in *Gulliver's Travels.* The sailor's rescue of Gulliver, the Brobdingnagian state, though it is not perfect, show the possibilities of goodness available to man. Swift rejected any idea of a revolution that can turn the world into a paradise but he always believed that the redemption of humanity was possible.

Gulliver is infatuated with the impossible rational perfection of the Houyhnhnms and hates mankind. But Swift says in one of his letters "I do not hate mankind" only *vous autres* have them "reasonable animals" and it is they who hate mankind for being disappointed. Realism about human nature cannot be described as pessimism. Only those who expect the impossible fall into misanthropy. Swift believes that man cannot transcend fully the Yahoo nature, though redemption of man is possible. It is also part of the Swiftean irony that Gulliver finds his utopia in the land of another species. Swift brings out the true nature of man in the image of the Yahoo and exposes the illusory pride of man viewed from this angle. *Gulliver's Travels* is not a satire on man but a satire on the idea, the belief in the perfection of man. It is necessary to understand Swift through the old-fashioned theological terms "degeneration of man." Only then it is possible to demolish the idea of Swift's misanthropy.

TRENDS OF THOUGHT IN THE EIGHTEENTH CENTURY

John Locke (1632-1704), the English Philosopher developed the doctrine of empiricism according to which knowledge was acquired by experience, not by intuition. In his book, *Reasonableness of Christianity* he expounded that Adam's fall brought punishment of death on man but it implies no corruption of human nature in posterity.

Thomas Hobbes (1588-1709) the English philosopher and political theorist in his book, *Leviathan* (1651) advocated absolute monarchy as the only means of controlling clashing human interests and desires and guaranteeing their rights of self-preservation and happiness. He believed men to be rational creatures.

Rene Descartes (1596-1650), the French philosopher and mathematician, often called the father of modern philosophy, introduced his technique of philosophical inquiry in his *Discourse on Method* (1637). He had a stoic faith in beneficent God and an uncorrupted nature and that reason is from God and must be trusted. He extolled pride against humility which was evil. For him man was a god. To follow God and reason was the stoic faith.

Michel de Eyquem Montaigne (1533-92), the French essayist believed that man was on a level with beasts. His *Apologie* is a scathing attack upon stoic pride where man is placed below the dog and the horse. Deism was a belief in god based on reason rather than revelation and involving the view that God has set the universe in motion but does not interfere with how it runs. Deism was especially influential in the 17th and 18th centuries.

Pelagius (360-420), Romano-British monk denies the existence of the original sin and believed that people can earn salvation through their own efforts, without relying on the grace of God.

St. Augustine (354-430) Roman priest and theologian was against stoicism in the form of Pelagian heresy. Pelagius was condemned as heretic.

6

THE CHAPTERWISE SUMMARY OF *GULLIVER'S TRAVELS* WITH COMMENTS

BOOK I

THE VOYAGE TO LILLIPUT

1

Lemuel Gulliver was the third of the five sons of his parents. He studies at Cambridge for three years and becomes apprentice to Mr. James Bates, an eminent surgeon in London for four years. He also learns navigation. On the recommendation of Mr. Bates, he becomes surgeon to the Swallow, a ship commanded by Captain Abraham Pannel. After a few years, he settles in London and attends patients. He marries Mary Burton second daughter to Edmund Burton, hosier in Newgate street. After the death of Mr. Bates, when he fails as a medical practitioner, he decides to go to the sea where he spends six years. He stays at home for three years and then accepts the offer of Captain William Prichard, master of the Antelope to make a voyage on the South Sea. They set sail from Bristol on May 4, 1699.

On their way to the East Indies, on November 5, the ship is driven against a rock by a violent storm. The crew along with Gulliver are now sailing in a boat which is overturned by a strong gale. Gulliver has no idea as to what happens to others. But Gulliver swims up to the shore and the storm is also abated. He reaches an island about eight o'clock in the evening. Under the effect of fatigue and drink, Gulliver immediately falls asleep. Next morning, when he tries to rise, he is unable to do so as his whole body is tied by strings to the pegs. When the sun is up, he feels something moving on his left leg and comes almost to his chin. He raises his head as far as he can to see. To his surprise, he finds a human creature but only six inches high with a bow and arrow in his hands and quiver at his back. Then forty more of the same size follow. Gulliver roars so loud that they jump to the ground out of fear. As he struggles, he is able to free his left arm. Gulliver gives a tug at the strings and feels more free. For the second time, they run out of fear as Gulliver turns his head. Then a hundred arrows are shot on his body as a great shout runs through them. He feels as if pricked by needless and groans with pain. Some try to pierce Gulliver with their spears. As he has his jerkin on his body, they have no effect on him. Gulliver frees himself completely with his left hand. The arrows stop as he is quiet. When he turns, he finds a stage of about a foot and a half from the ground with two or three ladders to mount it. There are four men on the stage. From the stage a person of quality makes a long speech but it is not intelligible to him at all. He orders and fifty men move to Gulliver and cut his strings. The principal is a middle aged man and taller and attended by three persons. Gulliver feels extremely hungry and repeatedly brings his hand to mouth demanding food. Their lord understands the hint and at his orders several ladders are applied to his sides and hundreds of men with buckets full of meat walk towards his mouth. Gulliver eats it up and makes a sign that he wants to drink. They bring water and he drinks it up. After some time, a person of high rank from the imperial majesty appears.

Five hundred carpenters and engineers make a frame of wood raised three inches from the ground about seven-foot long and four wide and moving upon twenty-two wheels. Gulliver is raised in his sleep on this wheeled frame and tied to it and drawn to the metropolis by fifteen hundred of the emperor's largest horses. Next day, after covering a distance of half a mile, Gulliver reaches there. The Emperor and the courtiers come out to meet him. Not less than ten thousand men apply ladders and mount on his body. They are restrained by a proclamation and Gulliver has to crawl into a temple where he is lodged.

Critical Comments

The very first chapter of the first book sets up Gulliver as a fictional character with his family background, education and marriage. Soon after establishing the objective identity of Gulliver as a character, the exact date of the voyage, the description of shipwreck, the perils at sea and Gulliver's adventurous escape to an island where men are only six inches high, suggest a realistic account of a real voyage in the true tradition of the voyage literature. But as Gulliver lands in a strange country where men are only six inches high and they appear like dolls to the giant size Gulliver, the symbolic dimension of the voyage is also obvious. Here Swift uses the device of minification of man through which, later on, he shows symbolically the smallness of man. The very fact that Gulliver has done no harm to them but he is tied to the ground by strings and is attacked by arrows and spears implies that the physical size of the people in Lilliput is the measure of their intellectual and moral size.

2

The emperor of Lilliput attended by several of the nobility comes to see Gulliver in his confinement. He surveys Gulliver with great admiration but from a distance. He orders his cooks and butlers to give him food and drink which are pushed forward in a sort of vehicles upon wheels. Gulliver takes these vehicles, empties them all, twenty of them containing meat and ten containing liquor. Gulliver empties the liquor of ten vessels in a draught. The emperor, the princes and princesses, present there are astonished at this sight.

The emperor is taller by almost the breadth of Gulliver's nail than any at his court. He has a strong and masculine features with an Australian lips and arched nose. His complexion is olive, his countenance erect, body and limbs well-proportioned and all his motions are graceful. On the whole, he is majestic in his dress, is very plain and simple. He has a light golden helmet on his head, adorned with jewels and a plume on the crest. He has a sword drawn in his hand to defend himself against Gulliver. The sword is almost three inches long, the hilt and scabbard are enriched with diamonds.

His voice is shrill and articulate. He tries to talk to Gulliver but fails.

When the court retires, Gulliver is left with a strong guard to keep watch on him. They are ordered to shoot Gulliver if necessary. Gulliver takes six guards in his right hand pretending to eat them and then releases them. As soon as they are released, they run away. He does the same with all of them. The kindness of Gulliver impresses the emperor and he orders to prepare a special bed for Gulliver who spent his nights on the ground.

The Emperor appoints a team of learned men to teach Gulliver their language and the emperor's horses and troups of guards exercise in front of him in order to accustom themselves to him. During three weeks, Gullivers makes a great progress in learning their language. During this period, the Emperor often visits him and is pleased to assist his masters in teaching him. Gulliver expresses his desire for liberty with the words he has learnt.

Gulliver's pockets are searched and his swords and pistols are taken away from him. The Emperor promises to return all his things when he leaves their country. The emperor is curious to see the watch of Gulliver and orders two of his men to bear it on a pole. He is amazed at the continual noise it makes and the motion of the minute hand. The spectacles of Gulliver escape detection as it is in the private pocket of Gulliver's coat. An inventory is prepared by the officials in the name of Quinbus Flestrin which in their language means "man-mountain."

3

The gentleness and good behaviour of Gulliver gains the favour of the Emperor, his court and the general people. The day the emperor has a mind to entertain himself with the country shows, such arrangements are made. When a great office falls vacant by death etc. by disgrace, several youths apply to the emperor for employment. They dance on the rope. One who jumps highest without falling gets the appointment. The chief ministers are commanded to show their skill to convince the emperor that they have not lost their skill. Flimnap, the treasurer and Reldrersat, the principal secretary for private affairs are skilled in the art. Similar diversions are arranged for the Emperor, the empress and the first minister. The emperor has six inch long silken threads of blue, red and green colours. The Emperor or the minister holds the stick in his hand. The candidates jump and move in keeping with the rhythm of the movement of the stick. One who performs the best gets the blue ribbon, the second best, the red ribbon and the third best, gets the green ribbon around his neck. All great persons wear their girdles.

One day Gulliver takes nine sticks of two feet each, fixes four of them in the ground in a quadrangular figure with the four others running parallel to them. Then he spreads his handkerchief over them, mounts a troop of twenty-four horses with officers. They get into order, divide into two parts, perform mock skirmishes, pursue, attack, retire and display their military skills. The parallel sticks prevent them from falling to the ground. The emperor is delighted very much with the show.

Gulliver applies many times for liberty. At last, the emperor discusses the matter in the cabinet and later places it before the council. It goes unopposed except by Skyresh Bolglam who chooses Gulliver as his enemy without any provocation. Finally it is confirmed by the emperor and the council in spite of his opposition. One minister, Galbet or Admiral of the Realm prevails to link up the liberty of Gulliver with a number of conditions, the articles of which Gulliver has to swear in the presence of Skyresh Bolgolam attended by two under secretaries. It is also decided after his release that he will be supplied meat and drink of 1928 Lilliputians because according to the calculation of the emperor's mathematicians so much food and drink is necessary for the Man-mountain of his size.

Critical Comments

The rope-dancings and jumpings in keeping with the pleasure of the emperor is the symbolic representation of the way one could pave his way to success in the English Court by acting like the circus clowns at the beck and call of the King. Flimnap, the Treasurer is Sir Robert Walpole who was the Prime Minister of England from 1715 to 1717 and then from 1721 to 1742. His dancing on tight-rope suggests his shrewd parliamentary tacts and skills. Reldresal represents Lord Carterel appointed by Walpole to the position of Lieutenant of Ireland. The red, green and blue ribbons with which the courtiers are rewarded also represent the awards instituted by Queen Anne in 1703, by George I in 1725 and the one bestowed upon Walpole in 1726 respectively.

4

The first request that Gulliver makes after his liberty is the permission to visit Mildendo, the Metropolis. It is granted on the condition that Gulliver will not hurt the inhabitants nor their houses. The wall around the Metropolis is two and a half-foot high and eleven inches broad, flanked by two towers at the distance of ten feet. Gulliver is allowed to walk on the main roads only and not to enter the streets. He finds the garret windows and tops of the houses are so crowded to see the Man-Mountain that it is the most populous city ever seen by him. The city is square, each side of the wall being five hundred foot long. The two streets that cross and divide into four quarters are five-foot wide. The lanes and alley's are twelve to eighteen inches wide. The town houses five hundred thousand people. The houses are three-storeyed or five-storeyed.

The palace of the emperor is in the centre of the city where the great streets meet. It is surrounded by a two-foot high wall at a distance of twenty feet from the building. The outside court is a square of forty feet and includes two other courts. The royal apartments are in the inside court. Gulliver cannot see them as the gates are eight inches high and seven inches wide. The building of the court is five-foot high. Gulliver makes two stools from the wood of the two largest trees that he cuts. He stands on the stool one by one, crosses the walls of the palace without damage and sees the magnificence of the palace. He lies down in the inner court and sets his eyes to the open windows of the middle storeys. He sees the empress and young princes in the apartments. The empress gives her hand through the window to kiss.

A fortnight after the liberty of Gulliver, Reldresal, Principal Secretary of Private Affairs comes to Gulliver's house attended by a servant. He wants to talk to Gulliver. Gulliver expresses his desire to lie down in order to give him audience but he prefers Gulliver to hold him in his hand during the conversation. He tells Gulliver about two struggling parties in the empire under the names of Tramecksan and Slamecksan from the high and low heels on their shoes which is their distinguishing mark. Though the High-Heels are agreeable to the constitution, the emperor employs only Low-Heels in the government and administration because the heels of the emperor are slightly lower than any at his court. The number of the High-Heels is larger than the Low-Heels. There is permanent enmity between these two parties. There is also a danger of attack from a neighbouring island of Blefuscu. The two kingdoms are in a state of war for the last thirty-six months. It began in this way. It was a primitive practice to break the eggs at the larger end but the present emperor's grandfather when he was a boy cut one of his fingers by breaking the egg according to the custom. Then his father, the emperor passed the order to break the egg on their smaller end. This order created such a great rebellion that an emperor lost his life and another his crown. Eleven thousand persons lost their life. The books on the subject published by the Big-Endians were banned and the emperors of Blefuscu charged Lilliputians of creating a division in religion and breaking a fundamental doctrine of the great prophet, Lustrog in the fifty-fourth chapter of Brundecral, their holy book which says that all their believers shall break their eggs at the convenient end. The Big-Endians exiles have found refuge and support of Blefuscu. So the war has continued for thirty-six months between the two kingdoms. They have lost forty ships, greater number of smaller vessels, thirty thousand seamen and soldiers. They have made numberless fleet and are preparing for an attack. The Emperor has great confidence in the valour and strength of Gulliver and has directed to communicate it to Gulliver. Gulliver replies he has a desire to serve the emperor. But as he is a foreigner, he does not want to interfere with their affairs. But he is ready to defend the emperor and his kingdom against a foreign invasion.

Critical Comments

This chapter deals with the metropolis of Lilliput and the second part of the chapter deals with the conversation between

Reldresal, Principal Secretary of Private Affairs and Gulliver about the affairs of Lilliput. The satirical element is remarkable in this chapter. Lilliput stands as the symbol of England. The dispute between the Big-Endians and the little Endians represents the theological hair-splitting between the Catholics and the Protestants. The dispute is held up to ridicule as it is based on petty considerations. Lilliput is England and Blefuscu is France. The dispute between Lilliput and Blefuscu represents the dispute between France and England. The High-Heels and the Low-Heels represent the Whig and the Tory parties and the petty politics in which they engage themselves. The details of this chapter contain veiled references to contemporary events and figures of the time as well as the smallness and pettiness of man.

5

The empire of Blefuscu is an island situated to the north-east side of Lilliput separated by a channel of eight hundred yards wide. As Gulliver comes to know the enmity between two kingdoms, he does not appear on this side of the sea-coast. When it is reported that the enemy's whole fleet is at an anchor in the harbour, Gulliver procures from the Lilliputians cables and hooks which are like threads and needles. Gulliver wades into the sea for half an hour and reaches the fleet. He ties the ships with cables and hooks and pulls the cords at the end. Gulliver has to face several thousand arrows on his face and hands. He takes care to save his eyes by putting on his spectacles. The ships do not move on being pulled. Gulliver then cuts the cables that anchor the ships. Though the enemies shoot thousands of arrows, Gulliver pulls behind him the whole fleet to the great disappointment of the inhabitants of Blefuscu. As Gulliver is neck-deep under water, the Lilliputians see only the fleet of enemy's ships advancing towards them. They do not see Gulliver. As he moves towards the shore, their fears are abated. The Emperor receives Gulliver with great admiration and confers upon him the highest life of honour, Nardac.

The emperor now wants Gulliver to bring all the ships of the enemy into his ports and reduce the whole empire of Blefuscu to a province to be governed through a viceroy. He wants to destroy the Big-Endians and become the monarch of the whole world. Gulliver dissuades the Emperor from his purposes from his sense of justice against enslaving a free people. But the Emperor cannot forgive him for opposing his plans. The matter is debated in the council. The emperor is opposed by the wise men except a few secret enemies of Gulliver. Since then some ministers have been bent on conspiring against Gulliver to destroy him. The services of Gulliver to the emperor are not taken into consideration.

Three weeks after the event the offer of peace comes from the kingdom of Blefuscu. The treaty of peace is concluded with great advantage to the emperor of Lilliput. The ambassadors of Blefuscu report to their emperor the favourable bent of Gulliver towards Blefuscu. As a result, Gulliver pays several visits to Blefuscu on invitation. Before returning to his own country, Gulliver requests the emperor of Lilliput to allow him to visit Blefuscu. It is granted reluctantly as Flimnap and Bolgolam have poisoned the ears of the emperor against Gulliver.

Once Gulliver is alarmed by the cries of several thousand people at midnight. Several of the emperor's courtiers rush through the crowd and request him to save the apartments of the empress in the palace which is on fire on account of the carelessness of a maid. Gulliver reaches the palace without trampling on the people. All efforts prove ineffective. Then Gulliver starts urinating on the burning part of the palace and in three minutes the fire is put out. It was a crime to urinate in the premises of the emperor's palace. So Gulliver is afraid. Gulliver receives a message from the emperor that he will request the judges to grant him pardon. But he fails to obtain pardon. The empress retreats from her own apartment to the most distant place in the palace and that part of the palace remains unrepaired.

Critical Comments

Gulliver in the fifth chapter of Book I becomes a hero by averting the possible attack of the neighbouring country, Blefuscu. He brings the enemy's fleet of ships to the port of Lilliput in the teeth of arrows flying against him. He is awarded with the highest title of Nardac. Although Gulliver is greatly honoured, he refuses to destroy Blefuscu completely. He argues for, and brings about a peace treaty between the warring sides. But the rising influences of Gulliver annoys Flimnap, the treasurer and Skyresh Bolgolam, the first lord of Treasury. They conspire against Gulliver and poison the ears of the emperor. Meanwhile, the royal palace catches fire. Gulliver puts it out by urinating on it. But the empress is annoyed with Gulliver for his fire-fighting technique.

The empress who harbours prejudice against Gulliver after extinguishing the fire in her apartment by urinating is Queen Anne who after the publication of *A Tale of a Tub* was suspicious of Swift and never considered him fit to hold the position of a bishop and he had to remain content with Deanery at St. Patrick's in Dublin. Bolgolam represents the Earl of Nottingham who used his influence to block Swift's promotion. Flimnap is Sir Robert Walpole who displayed his skill in the parliamentary and political intrigues. There is a close parallel between Gulliver and Lord Bolingbroke. Like Gulliver he brought an end to a long war between England and France. Like Gulliver he was condemned by his political opponents for not bringing about complete surrender of the enemy and was accused of culpable association with French ambassadors.

6

As the size of the Lilliputians is under six inches high, so their trees, plants and animals are proportionately small. Horses and oxen are four and five inches, the sheep, an inch and a half. Their tallest trees are seven-foot high. They write aslant from one corner of paper to another and bury the dead with their heads downward because by the time they will rise again, the earth will turn upside down. Crimes are dealt with severely. If the accused proves his innocence, the accuser is executed immediately and the innocent person is compensated out of his goods and lands. If found lacking it is supplied by the crown. Fraud is considered greater than theft and punished with death. The government hinges on reward and punishment. One who comes up with the evidence of observing the laws of the country for seventy-three months is rewarded with money and title of legal which is added not only to his name but his posterity.

In selection of people for employment, good morals rather than great abilities are considered. They think that a qualified person without morality cannot be trusted for duty and service. The mistakes of ignorance are less dangerous than moral corruption. Lack of belief in a Divine Providence renders a man incapable of holding a public position under the government. It is just the principle. In practice, jumping and rope-dancing leads to the postings on high ranks.

Ingratitude is considered a great crime and is punished with death. As parents cannot be trusted with the education of children, the children of both the sexes except those of cottagers and labourers are sent to school when they are twenty months old. Professors and their deputies look after them. They put on plain dress and are brought up on the principles of honour, justice, courage, modesty, religion and love of their country. They are in work also but not in times of eating and sleeping and get two hours for diversion. They are dressed by men upto the age of four and then they dress themselves. Parents meet the children twice a year. The visit lasts only an hour. They are allowed to kiss their children at meetings and partings. They bring no gifts. The tax for education is charged by the emperor's officer from each family. The children of traders are put to their trade at the age of eleven but the children of persons of quality study upto the age of twenty-one.

There is no difference between the education of boys and girls. The girls are dressed by the elderly women upto the age of five. Only girls are engaged in less robust exercises and they are given some rules of domestic life. Girls are married at the age of twelve. Their parents take them home with expressions of gratitude to professors. The girls of the meaner sort are instructed in all kinds of work and dismissed at nine years and the rest at thirteen years. The cottagers and labourers keep their children at home. They cultivate the land and their education is supposed to be irrelevant. The old and the diseased are taken care of by hospitals. Begging is unknown in the kingdom.

Two hundred semptresses are employed to make Gulliver's shirts and linen for his bed and table which he has carved out of the largest trees. Three hundred tailors are engaged to make his clothes. When the clothes are ready, they look like patchwork but of only one colour. Three hundred cooks prepare his food. Twenty waiters are put on the table to serve Gulliver. A hundred are on the ground with dishes of meat, wine and other things. A dish of meat is just a mouthful and so is the drink and wine.

One day the Emperor with the Empress and Princes and Princesses attended by Flimnap, the Lord high Treasurer comes to dine with Gulliver. They sit with their chairs on the table. Flimnap who caresses Gulliver more than is usual is the secret enemy of Gulliver. After this event, Flimnap advises the emperor to dismiss Gulliver because he is a burden on the exchequer. The treasurer, Flimnap also believes the rumour that his wife has an affair with Gulliver. But she always comes to Gulliver publicly with her sister and young daughter. Later the truth comes to light and the husband and the wife are reconciled.

Critical Comments

Gulliver here talks about the laws, customs and educational system of Lilliput. Some critics have discovered the influence of Plato and Thomas More's *Utopia* on this part. In principle moral rather than clever people are appointed to top positions and non-believers are debarred from public office. But in practice, flattery paves the way to high positions. The education of the Lilliputians are well-planned and students are trained in the values of life. The Lilliputians are good at practical mathematics. So unlike the Laputans, the clothes they prepare for Gulliver fit him well.

7

When Gulliver is preparing to pay a visit to the emperor of Blefuscu, an important person of the court (whom Gulliver has helped by using his influence with the emperor) comes one night secretly to Gulliver. As usual, Gulliver puts him in a chair on the table. He informs Gulliver that Skyresh Bolgolam who has been his mortal enemy hates him more after his success against Blefuscu which has dimmed his glamour as admiral. This Lord together with Flimnap, the High Treasurer has prepared the charges against Gulliver which are already approved by the Emperor. A copy of the charges is brought to Gulliver by this lord.

The first charge against the Mountain-Man is that on the pretext of extinguishing fire of the emperor's palace, he has urinated in the premises of the royal palace. It is against the law of the land. The second charge is that after bringing the fleet of Blefuscu into the royal port, he has refused to obey the orders of the emperor to destroy all the Big-Endians and reduce Blefuscu to a province of Lilliput on the ground that his conscience does not allow him to destroy the liberties of an innocent people.

The third charge relates to the fact that Gulliver has behaved with the ambassadors of Blefuscu with almost friendliness knowing well that they belong to a nation hostile to the emperor. The fourth charge is that it is unfaithfulness of Gulliver to prepare for a voyage to Blefuscu for which he has only verbal permission. He intends to make the journey to help the emperor of Blefuscu against the emperor.

During the debates the emperor argues that in view of the services of Gulliver to the Kingdom his crimes should be extenuated. But the treasurer and the admiral insist that he must die for his crimes. His house should be set on fire at night. He should be shot with poisonous arrows and he should be served food with poison. But the emperor is for sparing Gulliver's life. Then Reldresal, Principal Secretary of Private Affairs admits that the crimes of Gulliver are great but the mercy of the emperor is greater. Gulliver's life should be spared in view of his services to the kingdom but the emperor should be kind enough to put out his eyes only. This is opposed by Bolgolam, the Admiral. His opinion is that Gulliver who urinated in the compound of the palace might drown it. If he can bring the ships of the enemy, he can take them back also with his strength. He says that Gulliver is a Big-Endian in his heart and before he comes into action, he must be put to death. The treasurer points out the loss of treasury due to Gulliver. The Emperor and the council are convinced of Gulliver's guilt for which he deserves death. The secretary replies to the objection of the treasurer that Gulliver should be starved to death gradually and his skeleton be preserved as a monument for posterity. The putting out of the eyes is recorded in the book and starvation by degree is kept a secret.

The secretary will come to Gulliver and read out the articles of impeachment and stress the leniency of the emperor in taking out his eyes only for which the surgeon of the court will attend him. The important lord leaves him immediately to avoid suspicion and for Gulliver to decide his future course of action. Before the judgment is carried out, Gulliver informs the Secretary by the letter of his decision to visit Blefuscu. Gulliver goes to the seashore, catches a man of war, lifting up the anchor, wades to the royal port of Blefuscu.

Gulliver gets two guides to reach the capital of the city. The royal family and great officers come to receive him. As the emperor, the empress and the ladies get down the horses and coaches, Gulliver gets his down on the ground to kiss the hand of his Majesty and the empress. Gulliver tells the emperor that he has come to Blefuscu to do service if any to the kingdom. Gulliver is mistaken in his thought that the emperor will not discover the disgraceful events which led Gulliver to come to Blefuscu.

Critical Comment

This chapter dwells at length on the conspiracy hatched against Gulliver in the political circles which is a common feature of the petty politics in which the politicians engage themselves in countries ruled by monarchs and kings. The impeachment against Gulliver is a satire on the actual impeachment of four Tory ministers, Bolingbroke, Oxford, Ormonde and Strafford. Like Gulliver, Bolingbroke and Ormonde escaped to France. The kindness of the emperor which is overemphasized has an ironical reference to the executions which took place after the rebellion of 1715 and the praises of George I's mercy published by the government. Reldresal who remains a true friend of Gulliver represents Lord Carterel who was secretary of state from 1721 to 1724.

8

One day Gulliver observed a boat overturned in the sea. He asked the emperor of Blefuscu to lend him twenty of the tallest vessels and three thousand seamen. With their help, he is able to bring the boat to the royal port of Blefuscu. He requests the emperor of Blefuscu to provide him with materials to repair the boat and seeks his permission to depart which is granted.

Meanwhile a message comes from the emperor of Lilliput to the emperor of Blefuscu that Gulliver should be sent back to Lilliput on the ground that he has escaped from just punishment for his treason. Gulliver thinks of departing early so that he does not become a bone of contention between the two monarchs. When Gulliver is ready to depart, the emperor of Blefuscu presents him with a good number of gold coins and his own full length picture. He takes with him six cows and two bulls intending to propagate their breed in his own country. Gulliver sets out on the sea on 24 September, 1701. Having covered some distance, Gulliver catches sight of a ship. He signals to it and is quite delighted to find that it is an English ship. He boards the ship and shows his cows and sheep to the captain and the crew. He reaches England on 13 April, 1702. Gulliver makes considerable profit by showing his cattle to the people. He stays home for two months before he makes another voyage.

Critical Comments

This chapter brings to a close Gulliver's voyage to Lilliput. The strained relationship between the emperor of Lilliput and the emperor of Blefuscu regarding Gulliver is the symbolic representation of the relation between England and France where Bolingbroke had sought refuge.

Lemuel Gulliver's voyage to Lilliput is full of topical allusions to the contemporary England. But they are transmuted into the symbolic and allegorical caricature of the institutions of mankind and provides a mirror to man with all his smallness, pettiness and hypocrisy, though some aspects of the life of the Lilliputians are good, for example, their system of education.

BOOK II

THE VOYAGE TO BROBDINGNAG

1

Gulliver is a man of active life and restless nature. After two months' stay at home, on 20 June, 1762, Gulliver set out in the Adventure with Captain John Nicholas, a Cornish man being the commander. The ship is bound for Surat. They reach the cape of Good Hope and land for fresh water. The captain falls sick and they are able to leave the cape by the end of March. They pass the straits of Madagascar. The wind is violent in this region from December to May. The winds begin to blow with greater violence on April 19 and the ship is driven to the east of Molucca Islands. The winds stop in May and perfect calm prevails. But the captain, a man of experience forecasts a storm which overtakes them the next day. The fierce storm drives the ship about five hundred leagues to the east. The sailor is not sure in what part of the world they are. They need fresh water on 16 June, 1703. Land becomes visible on 17 June, 1703. They are in full view of the great island or continent. Part of the land jutted out into the sea. They cast anchor within a league of the creek and the captain of the ship sends a dozen of his men in a long boat with vessels for water. With the permission of the captain, Gulliver accompanies them. They are in search of water and Gulliver walks about to discover the rocky country. When Gulliver wants to return, he finds his companions already in the boat moving for life to the ship. He wants to call after them, when he finds a huge creature wading knee-deep in water after them in the sea. The monster is unable to catch them. Gulliver runs over the top of a hill and looks over the country which is fully cultivated. The length of the grass is twenty-foot high.

Gulliver follows a high road which is only a footpath through a field of barley. He finds himself amid forty-foot high crops and is unable to see anything. Gulliver reaches the end of a field which is fenced with 120 feet high hedge with four steps six-foot high and the upper stone above twenty. He sees through a gap in the hedge a man as tall as an ordinary spire-steeple moving towards the stile. Out of fear, Gulliver hides himself in the corns. The man crosses the stile, looks all about himself and calls his men in a voice loud as a trumpet. Seven giant-like men with harvest hooks in their hands appear who are his servants or labourers. They start reaping where Gulliver is hidden. As one of the reaper draws nearer to Gulliver, Gulliver for fear of being crushed in his next step, screams out. He carefully lifts Gulliver between his forefinger and thumb and looks at him at a distance of three yards. Gulliver is afraid of being dashed against the ground as we do with hateful little animals.

He puts Gulliver in the pocket of his coat and brings him to his master the farmer whom Gulliver has first seen in the field. He is amused to examine Gulliver carefully. The farmer and Gulliver do not understand each other's language. He takes Gulliver in the fold of his handkerchief. He shows Gulliver to his wife who screams as women do at the sight of a toad or a spider. In the noon, Gulliver is placed on the dinning table thirty-foot high from the ground with the farmer, his wife and three children and a grandmother. The ten-year old son of the farmer takes Gulliver by his left foot and lifts him in the air. The farmer beats his son but forgives him on the request of Gulliver.

The farmer's wife has a cat three times larger than ox in her lap. Gulliver is afraid of the cat but shows no sign of it. Dogs also come into the house but take no notice of Gulliver. A one year old child of the farmer takes the head of Gulliver in her mouth. Gulliver roars. She is afraid, drops Gulliver and starts crying. Then the mother gives her a suck. Gulliver is disgusted with the size, bulk, shape and colour of the breast and the nipple while he likes the same in his own country. After dinner, the farmers goes away leaving Gulliver to the care of his wife. She puts him into her bed and covers him with a handkerchief. Gulliver dreams he is in England with his family. He wakes up to find himself locked in the room with two rats of the size of a mastiff attacking him from two sides. Gulliver kills one of them and the other escapes. The mistress orders the maid to throw the dead rat through the window. She sets Gulliver on the table. He makes her understand he wants to stand on the floor. Then he goes with the mistress to the garden, hides himself and discharges the necessities of nature.

Critical Comments

The scale is transposed in Brobdingnag. In Lilliput, Gulliver was among the little dolls, in Brobdingnag where people are sixty-foot high, Gulliver is himself like a doll among the giants and the rest is adjusted on the same scale. The former was the parody of the human reality which the custom invests with grandeur, in Brobdingnag, the human reality reveals itself as ridiculous and infinitely small. Whereas the Lilliputians were hostile to Gulliver on his arrival, for no reason, Gulliver though he appears like an insect is treated kindly by the giant size people. So here Swift applies the focus of relativity to the reality through the technique of minification and magnification. In the two strange worlds, the physical size of the inhabitants represents their intellectual and moral size. The comic aspect of the satire also comes to light when the tiny Gulliver has to defend himself against rats.

2

The farmer's daughter is nine years old. She is good natured and forty-foot high. She treats Gulliver like a baby. She dresses and undresses Gulliver. She is skilled with her needle. She makes a number of shirts for Gulliver. She takes complete care of the needs of Gulliver. She calls Gulliver Grildrig and Gulliver calls her Glumdalclitch, the little nurse.

A friend of the farmer gives him the idea to exhibit Gulliver in the market-place as an object of curiosity against a small fee. The farmer along with his daughter takes Gulliver in a box to a neighbouring town on the market day. The farmer takes a large room of an inn where Gulliver is placed on a table. The farmer allows only thirty people at a time to see Gulliver in order to avoid crowding. As instructed by Glumdalclitch, Gulliver pays respects to the visitors, asks how they do and tells them that they are welcome. On the advice of his friend, the farmer along with his daughter takes Gulliver in a box riding a horse. Gulliver repeats his performance from town to town but gets extremely exhausted during the journey on the horse which goes about forty-foot at every step. But the farmer finds this business quite profitable and makes a lot of money. In this way, he reaches the metropolis on 26 October. The farmer takes a lodging in the principal street of the city not far from the royal palace. He hires a large room and exhibits Gulliver ten times in a day to the wonder and satisfaction of the people. Gulliver is now able to speak their language tolerably well and understand it perfectly well because Glumdalclitch in the leisure hours at home teaches him the alphabet and the language.

Critical Comments

This chapter gives an account of how the daughter of the farmer takes charge of Gulliver and he becomes an object of curiosity for his smallness of size. The report about this tiny man who was a Man-Mountain in Lilliput goes round that crowds gather to catch a glimpse of this freak of nature and ready to break the doors. The account seems quite realistic as the fatiguing effect of riding on Gulliver as well as the effect of his exhibition continuously is described with credible natural details. The reference to dates and months further render it realistic.

3

Gulliver loses his health on account of continuously entertaining the rabble in the house of the farmer. Meanwhile, the queen shows her interest in Gulliver and the farmer sells him for one thousand pieces of gold. Gulliver requests the queen to take Glumdalclitch into his service so that she may take care of him and instruct him. The queen agrees to this proposal and the girl also cannot conceal her joy. When the king looks at him, he takes him for a clockwork toy. When he finds Gulliver talking, he believes the circumstances by which he has come to the farmer's house and then to the court.

The scholars of the country after examining Gulliver agree that he is a freak of nature far inferior to other animals in swiftness, climbing trees, digging holes. He is also unable to defend himself. They cannot put him into the category of the dwarf as the queen's favourite dwarf, the smallest in the country is thirty-foot high. Gulliver argues that he comes from a country where there are several millions of both sexes of his status and animals, trees and houses are all in proportion, and they are able to defend themselves. The king calls the farmer, has a talk with him and is then satisfied that Gulliver's tale is true. He sets apart an apartment for Glumdalclitch at court whose duty is to look after Gulliver. The queen orders for making a box for a bed-chamber of Gulliver. At the direction, the wooden chamber of sixteen-foot square and twelve-foot high is ready with the window, a door and two closets. Two chairs and tables with a cabinet to put his things in are also made for him. The room is quilted to cushion any jolt in case of a fall from a high place. Gulliver is also supplied with clothes, blanket and a lock and a key.

The queen is so fond of Gulliver that she never dines without Gulliver in a chair with a table on the dining table. Glumdalclitch stands on a stool to take care of Gulliver. Silver dishes and plates and other things of Gulliver are kept by Glumdalclitch and taken out when requested. No one dined with Gulliver but her two daughters, one sixteen years old and another only thirteen years. The queen eats at one mouthful as much as a dozen farmers can eat. Her cups, knives spoons and forks are twice as big as a scythe.

On every Wednesday, the king, the queen, and the royal sons and daughters eat together in the queen's apartment and Gulliver joins them as their favourite. Gulliver talks to the Prince about his beloved country, its trades, wars, schism in religion, parties and politics. He takes Gulliver in his right hand and asks whether he is a Whig or a Tory. He expresses contempt at human grandeur which is mimicked by such dimunitive insects as Gulliver. The way he looks down upon human houses, cities, love and fight, disputes and betrayals, piety, honour, truth, pride and envy, the colour of indignation comes and goes several times on the face of Gulliver. Slowly Gulliver's fear of their bulk wearies off and he can look upon the English way of living as they do.

The queen's dwarf seeing a creature far beneath him becomes insolent with Gulliver. He seldom fails to remark about Gulliver's littleness and Gulliver calls him brother. One day he is so much irked by Gulliver's remarks that he catches Gulliver by the middle and puts him in a bowl of cream. Glumdalclitch takes him out. The dwarf is punished and given to a lady of high quality.

Flies of the size of a lark are numerous there. They hum and buzz and bite on the nose or forehead of Gulliver. Sometimes the dwarf catches them in his hand and lets them out under the nose of Gulliver. Gulliver cuts them to pieces with his sword to the great delight of the queen. The queen often asks Gulliver whether the people of his country are as coward as himself. One day Glumdalclitch puts his box on the window. Gulliver is eating the sweet cake. Twenty wasps attack him and try to eat. Gulliver fights back with his hanger. He kills four of them and the rest run away. They are large as patridges with their stings an inch and a half long and sharp as needles.

Critical Comments

This chapter shatters the grandeur of human pride as man is small as insects in comparison to the Brobdingnagians. Man appears exactly as the Lilliputians appeared to Gulliver. It is not just a matter of physical size. All the loves, hates, prides, wars are as petty and trivial as man himself. Though Gulliver provides amusement to the king, the queen and the maids of honour, the way he is attacked by rats, flies, monkeys appears quite comic.

4

Lorbrulgrud, the metropolis is about two thousand miles round. The whole extent of the Prince's dominion is about six thousand miles in length and from three to five in breadth. Gulliver suggests the geographers of Europe to correct their modern maps because they suppose nothing but sea between Japan and California.

The kingdom is a peninsula terminated to the north-east by a ridge of mountains thirty miles high which are impassable volcanoes. There is not a single sea-port. The country is well-inhabited as it contains fifty-one cities, one hundred walled towns and a great number of villages. The king's palace is a heap of buildings about seven miles round. The chief rooms are generally two hundred and forty-foot high and broad and long in proportion. The king's kitchen is indeed a noble building vaulted at top and about six hundred foot high.

Gulliver is always carried in his box which is large enough, though his governess often takes him out and holds him in her hand that he may more conveniently view the houses and the people as they pass along the streets. A smaller box was made for him for the convenience of travelling because the other is too large for his governess's lap. This travelling closet is an exact square with a window in the middle of the three of the squares and each window is latticed with iron and wire on the outside to prevent accident in a long journey.

Critical Comments

This chapter is purely descriptive. It gives an account of the metropolis of Brobdingnag. It is in keeping with the general size of the Brobdingnagian world. The houses, roads and streets are equally great and splendid. As usual, we are always aware of the smallness of the size of Gulliver in contrast to the gigantic size of people in Brobdingnag so that Gulliver is put in a wooden box or in the hand of his nurse to look at the outside world which otherwise remains hidden from his view. As this chapter forms just a part of the account of Brobdingnag, it adds to the realistic and authentic touch in the description of the entire kingdom and Gulliver in this brave new world. It leads a step forward to the satire of mankind where Gulliver, being a favourite of the queen and king, will bring the human world against the world of Brobdingnag in the following chapters.

5

The littleness of Gulliver brings many troubles to him. Once before the dwarf has left, he is teased by Gulliver. In return, he shakes the apple tree when Gulliver passes under it. Gulliver is flattened on the ground by the rain of falling apples. But the dwarf is pardoned as Gulliver has provided the provocation. The other day he is caught in hailstorm and beaten badly when he creeps under a lemon thorn. One day Glumdalclitch leaves Gulliver in the garden and goes to another part of the garden with her friends. In the meantime, the gardener's spaniel comes, catches him between his teeth and brings him before his master. Though Gulliver is not hurt, he is terribly afraid and cannot speak a word. The matter is not reported to the queen as his nurse is afraid of the queen. The kite once makes a swoop at him. Another time he falls into a mole-hill. The birds hop around him without being scared by his presence. A thrush also tries to snatch a piece of cake from him. One day Gulliver hits a linnet with a cudgel. He is struggling with the bird when a servant comes to his help and he has the linnet for his dinner.

The maids of Honour often invite Glumdalclitch to their apartments and desire her to bring Gulliver with her. They strip Gulliver naked from top to bottom and press him full length against their breasts on such occasions, Gulliver is disgusted with a foul smell from their skins. His sense is more acute in proportion to his littleness. But these maids are no more disagreeable to their lover than people of the same size are with people like Gulliver in England. The handsomest maid of Honour aged sixteen sets him astride upon her nipples. They strip themselves naked before Gulliver without any hesitation. Gulliver is displeased so that he requests his nurse to bring him away from that girl. Gulliver also sees the execution of a murderer with a forty-foot long sword.

The queen often talks to Gulliver when she finds him melancholy. Gulliver tells her that though he is a surgeon by profession, many times he is forced to work like a common mariner. Then Her Majesty gets a boat made under her instructions within ten days which can hold ten Europeans at a time. She puts the boat with Gulliver in it in a cistern for a trial where he cannot manage with his oars for want of room. She, then, orders to make a wooden trough of three hundred feet long and fifty broad and eight deep. Gulliver entertains the queen and her ladies with his skill and agility. Glumdalclitch takes the boat in the closet after boating is over. Once Gulliver slips down from the hand of the governess while being put to the boat. But he is saved as the corking pin sticks in the gentlewoman's stomacher. One day a frog of a huge size enters the trough from water and climbs up the boat with his full weight. Gulliver rushes to the opposite end to save the boat from being unbalanced. It jumps and leaps on Gulliver. Gulliver beats it with his oar and forces it out of the boat.

Once Glumdalclitch locks Gulliver in the closet and goes away. As it is hot, the closet window and the window of Gulliver's box are left open. A monkey of a clerk comes in through the window of the closet. He drags Gulliver out of the box through his paws. He catches him in the forefoot and holds Gulliver in the manner of giving a suck. When he hears the sound of the opening of the closet, he jumps to the roof of the next house with Gulliver. The monkey also thrusts victuals in his mouth from time to time. When the monkey is cornered by the people who apply ladders, he gives up Gulliver on a ridge tile, giddy with fear. One of the nurse's lads puts Gulliver in his pocket and brings him down. The stuff crammed down his throat is taken out with a needle. But Gulliver is so bruised and squeezed that he is confined to bed for a fortnight. The monkey is killed and no such animal is allowed inside the palace. The king, the queen and all the court come to enquire after his health during his sickness. Gulliver tells the king there are no monkeys in Europe except those brought to satisfy curiosities. They are so small that he can deal with a dozen of them together. At this, the king and others laughed at Gulliver's bravado as a person of low birth is laughed at by the greatest persons of the kingdom when he assumes importance.

Critical Comments

The entire chapter is comic and satirical. The littleness of Gulliver is his great disadvantage. The dwarf, the frog, the kite, rats and the monkey all prey upon Gulliver and he is himself generally unable to protect himself. He rows in a wooden trough, amuses the king and the queen and becomes their favourite. They take care that Gulliver is not hurt by them and enquire after his health in his illness. The climax of this satirical chapter is the laughter of the king and others at Gulliver's description of his bravado against monkeys etc. in his own country. Gulliver is made aware of his difference with the Brobdingnagians through this laughter. Moreover, the maids of honour strip him and themselves in his presence but Gulliver is disgusted with the smell and size of the parts of their bodies.

Gulliver picks up forty or fifty strongest stumps of hair from the barber of the king. He takes a fine piece of wood, makes holes in it at equal distance and fixes the stumps of hair in the holes. Thus he makes a fine comb. He combs the queen's hair and orders the cabinet maker to make two chair frames and holes at proper places and weaves the chair with the strongest hair like cane chairs in England. He presents the chair to the king. He also makes a purse in the same manner and with the queen's consent gives it to Glumdalclitch.

Gulliver attends musical concerts at the king's court frequently. But he keeps a distance from the performers because they sound like the trumpets of the army. There is a sixty-foot long spinet in the closet of Glumdalclitch. Gulliver wants to play upon it to entertain the king and the queen. He can reach only five keys, each being a foot wide. Gulliver makes two round sticks with a thick end each. He covers the thicker end with the mouse's skin. He runs fast on the bench playing upon the spinet and pleases the royalty.

The king frequently orders Gulliver to be brought with his box and to be put on the table. He, then, orders Gulliver to sit in his chair on the top of the cabinet which brings him to a level with the king's face. One day, the king orders Gulliver to give him an exact account of the government of England. Gulliver says that there are mighty kingdoms under one sovereign on two islands. He speaks of the House of the Peers as part of the English Parliament. Persons of the noblest blood and ancient and ample patrimony are members of the House. Special care is taken of their education in arts and arms as they become counsellors to the king, and members of the highest court of Judicature. Their honour is the reward of their virtue from which their posterity is not supposed to degenerate. Bishops are selected for the sanctity and purity of their life and education. The other part of the parliament is called the House of Commons. The members of this house are selected by the people for their abilities and love of the country.

Gulliver, then, explains how the court of Justice decides disputes of right over properties as well as punishment for vice. The king hears everything with great attention. He also makes some notes. He asks about the qualifications and quality of several officials and whether bribing is possible in appointments and judgments of disputes and whether voters can be purchased with money. He wants to know people who are bent upon getting into this assembly going through a lot of expense and trouble and later try to compensate for their trouble at the cost of the public good. He also inquires, whether it is possible to influence the judgment by the party in power and whether the lawyer argues for or against similar case and is paid for the service.

Gulliver tells him about taxes, population, the police, the army, war, religion and politics. He reports to the king a heap of conspiracies, rebellions, murders, massacres, revolutions, banishments, avarice, hypocrisy, perfidiousness, cruelty, rage, madness, hatred, envy, lust, avarice, during the last one century. The king tells Gulliver that he concludes that ignorance, idleness and avarice are qualifications of a legislator and that laws are best explained by those who are interested in confounding them. He compares his notes and says that it does not appear that priests, soldiers, judges, senators get their jobs for their virtue. He opines that as Gulliver is mostly on voyages, he has escaped the vices of his country and the conclusion he reaches is that the nations of England and Europe are "the most pernicious race of odious little vermin that nature ever suffered to crawl upon the surface of the earth."

Critical Comments

This is one of the most important chapters of Book II where the satire is directed against the civilized mankind. As Gulliver comes closer to the king, he gives him an account of the political, administrative and judicial system operating in England. From time to time, the king interrupts, raises his objections and points out possibilities of corruption and injustice in the system which runs in the country of Gulliver. It becomes transparent that the physical size of Gulliver as well as of the gigantic people of Brobdingnag has symbolic significance. The giants of Brobdingnag are also intellectual and moral giants and the human world of Gulliver is a world of moral and intellectual pigmies. The king holds the opinion that English history is nothing but the history of rebellions, revolutions, wars, crimes, avarice, fraud, deceit ambition and crimes. His conclusion is that the English people are nothing but "the most pernicious race of little odious vermin that nature ever suffered to crawl upon the surface of the earth."

Gulliver's account of his country before the King is marked by partiality. Though the king puts a number of questions, Gulliver tries to hide the frailties and deformities of his country and presents her in favourable light as far as possible. As the king is acquainted with the ways of the world, his notions of the vices and virtues are different from the polite centres of Europe. Gulliver attributes the king's criticism of England and Europe to his narrowness of thinking and his prejudices. In order to find favour with the king Gulliver tells the king of the invention of a powder which if kindled with fire blows even a mountain with more than the sound of thunder. This powder can at once destroy an army, the strongest walls, ships, houses and whole cities. Gulliver claims to know how to make and use the powder. He can destroy the whole metropolis if it chooses to disobey the king.

The king was struck with horror how a small insect like him can entertain such inhuman ideas, unmoved by the scenes of destruction he himself paints. Only an enemy of mankind could invent such things. Though the king likes discoveries in art and nature, he is ready to lose half his kingdom rather than share such an ignoble secret. He orders Gulliver not to mention such things in future. According to Gulliver, this attitude of the king is "the example of narrow principles and views. No European prince would have such a nice unnecessary scruple and let slip an opportunity of becoming the master of the lives, the liberties and fortunes of his people." The king is ignorant of the science of politics as found in Europe and the Europeans will form a poor opinion of the king. When Gulliver mentions books on the art of governance in his country, he has a low opinion of Europeans. He does not understand intrigues in the prince or secrets of the state when there is no enemy. His opinion is that whoever could make two ears of corn or blades of grass grow where only one did would deserve better of mankind than all the race of politicians put together.

The learning of the people is very defective as they know only morality, history, poetry and mathematics in which they excel. They have no concepts, ideas, abstractions and transcendentals.

The king's library is the biggest one with a thousand books. Gulliver, on examination, finds the style clear, masculine and smooth but not florid and economical of words. There is a book in Glumdalclitch's bedchamber about the weaknesses of humankind. Man is considered small, contemptible, helpless creature against weather and beasts. Other creatures excel man in strength, speed, foresight and industry. Nature degenerates gradually and the originally giant-like man grows smaller in size.

The king's army is made of tradesmen in cities and farmers in country and the noble and gentry being commanders without pay or reward. Gulliver once observes the military of Lorbrulgrud exercising in a great field near the city of twenty miles square. The horsemen are about one hundred feet high. They brandish their swords at once. Gulliver is surprised that the king has army when the country is not accessible from any side. The fact is that they are also troubled with the common disease of mankind. The nobility contends for power, people contend for liberty and the king for absolute power and so there have been civil wars also. Ever since the time of the civil war in the king's grandfather's time, the military has been kept with common consent.

Critical Comments

This chapter exhibits brilliant use of irony by Swift. Gulliver, an English and European man boasts of the invention of the gun-powder and the destructive uses to which it can be put. The king's humane attitude is described by Gulliver as "narrow outlook" and the result of prejudice and lack of the knowledge of the civilized way of living. The king's horror of the bloodshed and destruction that the gunpowder can bring about Gulliver attributes to unnecessary scruples. Here we find the terrible force of irony which exposes the upside down values of the English, European or human world. The king believes common sense, reason and justice as the basis of administration and he also presents the ideal quality of man to be his ability to increase production rather than to indulge in politics.

Gulliver has spent more than two years with Glumdalclitch in Brobdingnag. Now Gulliver wants to escape to the world of the people of his own size. He gets an opportunity. He along with Glumdalclitch accompanies the king and queen in their trip to the south coast of the kingdom. As usual, Gulliver is carried in his box which has silken ropes fixed from the four corners as a hammock. He sleeps on the hammock during the journey. The king stays in a palace near the seacoast. Glumdalclitch is fatigued and so the page accompanies Gulliver when he wants to take the fresh air of the sea. Glumdalclitch hands over Gulliver to the the page but bursts into a flood of tears as if she knows what is to come.

Gulliver casts a wistful glance towards the sea and takes a nap on the hammock. The boy shuts the window to keep out the cold wind and goes out to the rocks in search of birds' eggs. Suddenly Gulliver wakes up with a sudden pull on the hook of the box. He feels the box lifting up in air and borne forward with great speed. He cries aloud in vain. Through the window he can see only the clouds and the sky. He hears the clapping of wings over his head. He discovers some eagle has got the hook of his box in his beak. The flutter of wings suddenly increases and then Gulliver feels falling perpendicularly down for a few minutes. The box seems to splash on the surface of the water. Gulliver sees through the window that he has fallen on the sea and the box is floating on water. Gulliver can guess two or more eagles attacking the eagle with the box. The box falls down in the struggle. In this misfortune Gulliver remembers Glumdalclitch, feels the pang of separation and the grief she may have suffered. The two strong staples fixed on the side of the box has no window. Gulliver hears some grating noise on that side and then the box is towed on the sea. Gulliver peeps through the holes of the box, cries for help in a loud voice, fastens his handkerchief to the stick and waves it through the window several times.

The box of Gulliver strikes against something hard. Gulliver hoists his handkerchief again and calls for help. Then he hears a voice in English and says that he is an Englishman. Gulliver's box is tied to the ship. The box was put into the cabin of the captain. The box is cut and through a ladder Gulliver enters the ship. The captain treats him kindly. He had seen the handkerchief of Gulliver and come to his help. But Gulliver has difficulty in accustoming his eyes to the pigmies before his eyes. Gulliver relates all his adventures to the captain who comes to believe it only after he sees with his own eyes the things of Brobdingnag in possession of Gulliver. Gulliver reaches England on 6 June, 1706. The houses, men and trees and appear like those in Lilliput. Gulliver has difficulty in adjusting himself to the world of little men after his experience with giants in Brobdingnag. Like the captain of the ship, his wife and others consider him mad but they later understand him rightly. His wife advises never to go to the sea. But he does not accept the suggestion as we find later.

Critical Comments

In this chapter Swift winds up Gulliver's journey to Brobdingnag and his return to England with almost realistic and authentic account of little details that constitute the series of events that bring Gulliver back to his own country, England.

BOOK III

1

Gulliver sets out on his voyage again on 5 August, 1706. After ten days' journey, Gulliver's ship is chased by pirates. Gulliver and his friends are tied by strong ropes. One of the pirates is a Dutchman. He orders them to be tied back to back and thrown into the sea. Gulliver begs him to take some pity on them as they are Christians and protestants of neighbouring countries. It enrages him and he speaks to his companions in the Japanese language.

A Japanese captain who speaks a little Dutch, puts several questions and assures they will not die. Gulliver makes the captain a low bow and tells the Dutchman that he is sorry to find more mercy in a heathen than in a brother Christian. This makes them angry and it is decided that Gulliver should be set adrift in a little canoe.

After five days, Gulliver reaches an island which is all rocky, a little intermingled with tufts of grass and sweet-smelling herbs. There he gathers plenty of eggs upon the rocks and a quantity of dry sea-weed for his meal. He feels desolate and wonders how impossible it is to preserve his life in such a desolate place. He observes a vast body between himself and the sun moving towards the island. It seems about two miles high and hides the sun for six and seven minutes. As it moves closer over the place where Gulliver is, it appears to be a solid substance. He is amazed to discover a number of people moving up and down on that substance.

The appearance of human beings gives him a hope for life. The natural love for life fills him with joy and he is convinced that this adventure may help him out of this desolate place and condition in which he finds himself. Gulliver, waves his cap and handkerchief towards the flying island. But the trouble is that neither he can understand their language nor they make signs for him to come down. They let down the chain from the lowest gallery with a seat fastened to the bottom to which Gulliver fixes himself and is drawn up by pulleys.

Critical Comments

Just like Book I and Book II Gulliver introduces us to another marvel in Book III. This marvel is a flying island which is the product of scientific ingenuity. It is the product of Swift's inventive imagination which reflects the fact that Swift was far ahead of his times and could imagine aeroplanes in the form of flying islands two centuries ago.

When Gulliver reaches there, he is astonished at the singular shapes, habits and countenance of the people. Their heads are either reclined to the left or the right. One of their eyes is turned inside and the other upwards to the zenith. Their garments are adorned with suns, moons, stars, fiddles flutes, guitars, harps, trumpets and other musical instruments unknown to Europe. They have the custom of keeping servants with a blown bladder tied to a stick in their hands which contains dried peas. The servants flap on their mouth, eyes or ears to remind them to make use of them, because they are always absorbed in speculations. They attend their masters in their walks as being in deep thought, they may strike against a post and jostle against others in the street.

They take Gulliver to the top of the island and from there to the palace. Going upstairs many times, they forget what they are about till they are roused by their flappers. The king is flanked by persons of quality. There is a large table filled with globes, spheres and mathematical instruments. As the king is absorbed in a problem for an hour, he turns his attention to Gulliver on being gently struck by flaps in the hand of the servant. When the king speaks to him, a young man comes with a flap and gently flaps Gulliver on the ear. Gulliver, through signs, explains to them that he needs no such flappings. When it is discovered that Gulliver neither understands their language nor is he understood by them, he is sent by the king to an apartment in his palace. He has two attendants and Gulliver has the honour to dine with four persons close to the king. The servants cut bread into cones, cipher, parallelograms and several other mathematical figures.

After dinner, a person is sent by the king to teach Gulliver their language. Soon Gulliver is able to form sentences. He finds that the meaning of Laputa is the flying or floating island. The tailor comes and takes the measure of his body by describing the dimension of the whole body. But the dress does not fit his body. Gulliver goes to court in his new dress. He is now able to understand their language. The king orders to move down to Lagado, the metropolis of the kingdom upon the earth. It takes four days and a half. The next day, the king, attended by officers, plays music for three hours because the people of the island are adapted to hearing the music of the spheres. The king then orders the island to stop over villages and towns to receive petitions from them. Their language consists of scientific and musical phrases. They describe even the beauty of a woman through circles, parallelograms and geometrical terms. The houses are not well-built without one right angle in the wall. They have contempt for practical things. They are strangers to imagination, feeling and invention. They are interested in news and politics. They are mentally disturbed by apprehension from changes in the celestial bodies. For example, the earth may be consumed by the sun. The tail of a comet may strike the earth to pieces. The sun is continually spending its rays and it may lose all its rays. As a result, the earth and all other planets getting light from the sun may be destroyed. Their conversation revolves round such subjects and their sleep is disturbed by such apprehensions.

The women in Laputa are full of vivacity. They are fond of strangers and have contempt for their husbands. The women can indulge freely with their lovers in the presence of their husbands when they are absorbed in their speculation or unattended by their flappers. A court lady married to the Prime Minister goes down to Lagado on the excuse of health and remains there with a footman. She is brought back by the orders of the king but slips out to the same lover with her ornaments. The king has no interest in government, history, religion and manners of other countries. His interest is confined to mathematics and music.

Critical Comments

The chapter three of the Book III of *Gulliver's Travels* describes Gulliver's voyage to the flying island of Laputa where the king and the people are always absorbed in philosophical and scientific speculations. They are reminded by their servants to use their senses when the time comes to see, hear and speak. Their thoughts and conversations revolve round the movement of the sun, the moon, the comets and stars. They are not interested in practical matters. Quite symbolically, their one eye is turned inward and another to the sky. It presents Swift's imagination of philosophical and scientific world where man's mind is dominated by science, mathematics and music and they are strangers to imagination and fancy. The result is that their houses are clumsy, the clothes stitched for Gulliver after proper measurement hangs loose on his body and women can make love to others when the husbands are absorbed in speculation.

Laputa, the flying or floating island, is circular about four miles and a half. There is a sloping surface from the circumference to the centre so that the rain and the dew are collected in four large basins. The water is evaporated by the sunlight in the daytime. It is in the power of the monarch to raise the island above clouds and vapours and, thus, prevent rain and dew falling on the island.

At the centre of the island, there is a chasm about fifty yards in diameter from which the astronomers descend into a larger dome which is called the astrologer's cave situated at the depth of a hundred yards beneath the upper surface of the adamant. The place is equipped with twenty lamps, sextants, quadrants, telescopes, astrolabs and other instruments. The most strange thing is the loadstone of an enormous size, six yards in length. This magnet is sustained by a very strong circle of adamant passing through its middle upon which it plays and is poised so exactly that the weakest hand can turn it.

The island is made to rise and fall and move from place to place through the loadstone. It controls the movement of the island by means of the magnet attached to it. The island cannot move beyond the extent of dominions below nor can it rise above the height of four miles as the power of magnet cannot go beyond it. The loadstone is under the care of astronomers who regulate the movement of the island according to the direction of the monarchs.

The astronomers spend part of their time in observing celestial bodies through telescopes which are much more powerful than our own. So they are far advanced in their astronomical discoveries than their counterparts in Europe. They have discovered stars and satellites near Mars and ninety three different comets.

If the town is in revolt, the king punishes them by keeping the island hovering over it and deprives them of sunlight and rain and afflict them with dearth and disease. Sometimes stones are rained down on houses and people. If the king desires, he can drop the island on the town and bring about complete destruction. But, generally, the king does not prefer this course also because the bottom of the flying island may be damaged by rocks and other harder things. Once the people of Lindalino, another city in the kingdom revolted against the king, the flying island was commanded to be lowered up on the city. But as the people of Lindalino had already four towers with magnets, the island was pulled down with great force. The king realized the danger and yielded to the demand of the city.

Critical Comments

This chapter brings to light the indifference of the Luputans to the practical matters of life and complete absorption in scientific and philosophical speculation. The elaborate description of the factors that the scientists apply to regulate the movement of the flying island suggests the scientific and technological advancement of Laputa. It expresses Swift's distaste for the new learning. As some critics have pointed out, the flying island stands for England and the country below is Ireland. The way the king treats the people below represents the treatment of Ireland by the English politicians.

Gulliver is weary of staying on the same island. He finds himself neglected as the people are interested only in music and mathematics. They are far superior to Gulliver in both. One day, Gulliver requests a great lord at court to allow him to leave. The lord is quite dull but important because he is related to the king. On the 16th February, Gulliver leaves for Lagado, the metropolis with a letter of recommendation from the lord to his friend there. The entire continent of the flying island is called Balnibarbi and the metropolis, Lagado. Gulliver presents the letter to the lord's friend, Munodi who sets apart a part of the house for Gulliver during his stay. Munodi was, at one time, governor of Lagado. Though discharged on the ground of inefficiency, the king treats him with tenderness.

Here Gulliver finds houses clumsy and people in rags and employed in streets and fields in hard labour. But it is difficult to make head and tail of their labour. One day Munodi takes Gulliver to his country house. During his journey, Gulliver cannot understand the method of their farming because neither corn nor grass is visible. But on the estate of Munodi, it is a beautiful country with noble houses, corn-fields and trees. But the countrymen ridicule Munodi for managing his affairs in no better way. The house of this man is well made with fountains, gardens and avenues. Gulliver admires everything. In the night, he tells Gulliver he wants to destroy the present country and town and remodel them after his own ideas. But he fears the displeasure of the king and the people.

He tells Gulliver that forty years ago that certain persons went to Laputa who acquired little mathematics but came back full of spirit to put all arts, sciences and mechanics on a new footing. For this purpose, they set up an academy of projectors in Lagado. The professors in the college contrive new rules and methods of agriculture and building instruments and tools for trades and manufacturers whereby one man will do the work of ten. They are interested in projects of building houses to last forever, ripening fruits when you want and extracting sunbeams from cucumber and such happy proposals. As they have not succeeded in their projects, the whole country is laid waste, houses are in ruins, people, without food and cloth. But instead of being discouraged, they are all the more bent on prosecuting the schemes. Gulliver's host is a man of different spirits. He is content to live in the house of his ancestors. A few people like him have done the same and are looked upon with contempt as enemies to art and ignorant.

Gulliver wants to see the academy. He desires to see the ruined building on a mountain about three miles from his house. Lord Munodi tells him he had a very convenient mill within half a mile of his house, turned by the currents of a larger river sufficient for his family. But seven years ago, the group of projectors came with the proposal to destroy it and rebuild another on the side of the mountain by cutting a large canal and applying pipes and engines. He had to comply with the proposal under the pressure of circumstances. Hundred men worked for the plan but the plan was not successful. The projectors went laying the blame entirely on him. They railed at him and set others on the same plan with equal assurance of success and resultant disappointment. He is not on good terms with projectors. He recommends Gulliver to his friend to accompany Gulliver at the Academy.

Critical Comments

This chapter of Book III seems to be a satire in the form of allegory on the Royal Society with its projects of scientific investigation. As the fruits of such experiments were not visible immediately, Swift directs his satire against wasting time in fruitless experiments. But almost all the projects of the academy are not the inventions of Swift's imagination but mostly result of his study of the projects of the royal society. The experiments are highly ambitious and the experiment of inventing an instrument by which one man can do the work of ten men comes very close to our modern invention of computer. Swift's attitude to the science of his day who was opposed to it and favoured orthodox ways of working is reflected in the creation of a figure like Lord Munodi and his useful traditional methods of farming and building etc. against the new methods of working which bears little fruit.

Gulliver is permitted to visit the Grand Academy of Lagado. The Academy is not a single building, but a continuation of several houses on both sides of the street. There are many projectors engaged in their projects. The first projector that Gulliver meets has been engaged eight years for extracting sun-beams from cucumbers. These sunbeams are to be put into hermetically sealed vials and let out to warm the air in the cold weather.

Gulliver observes that another projector is engaged in an operation to convert excrement into the original food by separating several parts removing the tincture which it receives from the gall, making the odour evaporate and scumming off the saliva. One of the projectors who is called a universal artist is engaged with his fifty students in the improvement of human life. Some of his students are condensing air into a dry tangible substance. Some of them are softening marble for pillows and pin-cushions. Others were petrifying the hoofs of a living horse to preserve them from decay and the artist himself is busy on great designs. The first is to sow land with chaff and the second is to prevent the growth of wool upon two young lambs by applying outwardly a certain composition, gums, minerals and vegetables.

Another Professor is employed in a project for speculative knowledge by practical and mechanical operation. By this method, the most ignorant person can write books in philosophy, poetry, politics, law, mathematics and theology. In the school of language the first project is to shorten discourse by cutting pollysyllables into one and leaving out verbs and participles. The reason is that, in reality, all things imaginable are but nouns. They have also a scheme for entirely abolishing all words. In their opinion, as words are only names for things it will be more convenient for people to carry such things as were necessary to express their thoughts.

Critical Comments

This chapter is a satire particularly on every kind of impractical scholarship and the vain philosophy. Here Swift attacks the absurd and pretentious schemes of projectors and their stupidity. It shows that in Swift's opinion, these projects are purely waste of time and labour. But this chapter is not the pure invention of Swift's fertile satiric imagination. As modern researchers have pointed out except for two projects, all the projects of the Grand Academy are based on *The Philosophical Transactions* of the Royal Society which really existed in Swift's time.

2

Gulliver visits the school of politics where projectors are wholly out of their senses. They are proposing schemes for persuading monarchs to choose favourites on the basis of wisdom, capacity and virtues, for teaching ministers to consult the public for rewarding merit and ability and for choosing persons for employment who are properly qualified.

A doctor is engaged in finding out effectual remedies for all diseases and corruptions of public and administration so that their vices and infirmities may be corrected, of administrators as well as the people. This doctor proposes that on the meeting of a senate, certain doctors should be on duty for the first three days of their sitting and at the close of each day's debate to feel the pulses of every senator. On the basis of their diagnosis, they should administer to each legislator the kind of medicine to keep him mentally fit.

The highest tax is proposed upon men who are the greatest favourite of the other sex. Wit, valour and politeness are likewise proposed to be largely taxed. The women are to be taxed according to their beauty and skill in dressing. It is proposed in the interest of the crown that the members to be employed should take an oath to vote in favour of the court whether he wins or loses so that they impute their disappointments to fortune rather than to broken promises. Another professor shows Gulliver a large paper of instructions for discovering plots and conspiracies against the government. He advises great statesmen to examine the diet of all suspected persons, their time of eating, their digestion and form a judgment of their thoughts and designs.

Gulliver tells him that in the kingdom of Tribna where he has sojourned in his travels, people are discoverers, witnesses, informers, accusers, prosecutors all under ministers of state and their deputies. The plot in that kingdom is generally the work of the people who want to rise as politicians by pretending to restore new vigour to a crazy administration and thus try to fill their pockets. The suspected people in the state are accused of a plot and then put in chains. Their letters and papers are given to experts for examination and report. The professor is grateful to Gulliver for communicating these observations and promise to mention his name in his treatise. Gulliver is now thinking of returning to England.

Critical Comments

In this chapter, Swift mentions some more nonsensical and ridiculous investigations by the professors of Lagado. Swift makes fun of the professors who suggest that the physician should attend the politicians to keep them mentally fit and propose different nonsensical and illogical ways of raising funds and making money. Here Swift expresses his extreme bitterness against the politicians who are self-centred and who impose tax on the people for their personal gains.

This chapter is, in fact, directed against every kind of impractical and pretentious schemes of economists and promoters of English politics of the eighteenth century.

3

Gulliver leaves Lagado in order to return to Europe and arrives at the port of Maldonada. The town is very large. From here Gulliver makes a short trip to the little island of Glubbduldrib, the island of magicians. The tribes marry among each other and the elder in succession is the Prince or governor.

Gulliver is allowed to see the governor. When he goes to the governor, he is amazed to see how his highness dismisses all his attendance with turn of his fingers. He has the honour to dine with the governor where a new set of ghosts serve up meat and wait on the table. Gulliver stays there for ten days in that island. One night the governor tells him to call up whatever person he will choose to name and in whatever numbers among all the dead from the beginning of the world to the present time and to command them to answer any questions. Gulliver desires to see Alexander the great, Brutus and Caesar etc. Gulliver chiefly feeds his eyes on the destroyers of tyrants and usurpers and the restorers of liberty to the oppressed nations.

Critical Comments

According to Swift, it is impossible to say how far historic researchers are correct. Swift suspects the authenticity of historic researches as can be seen in the light of the information given by Alexander's ghost. It is said that Alexander was poisoned but his ghost informs that he "died of a fever of excessive drinking." The chapter also includes a satire on the people who believe in necromancy. Thus by calling up the spirits of the dead through magic he contradicts the truth as stated by historians. So here Swift points out the confusions that block the path of historical research.

4

Gulliver expresses his desire to the governor to see some of those ancient personalities who are renowned for wit and learning. He first desires to see Homer and Aristotle. They appear at the command of the governor. Gulliver recognises them easily. Aristotle freely accepts his mistakes in natural philosophy because it has proceeded in many things upon conjecture. Aristotle predicts that new systems of nature are new fashions which will vary in every age and be out of vogue when it is determined.

Gulliver is chiefly disgusted with modern history. He is surprised to find how the world is misled by prostitute writers to ascribe the greatest exploits in war to cowards, the wisest counsel to fools, sincerity to flatterers, the innocent and excellent persons condemned to death and banishment by the corruption of judges and ministers. He is also amazed to discover that perjury, oppression, fraud and panderism and like infirmities had important role in moulding the history of mankind. Gulliver also comes to know through his communication with the spirits of the dead that those who ought to be treated with great respect for their sublime dignity are considered inferior. Gulliver also talks to the spirit of a youth of about eighteen years. He tells Gulliver that he had been commander of a ship in the fight of Actium, broke through the enemy's line of battle, sank three of their ships and took a fourth which was the only cause of Antony's flight and the victory that followed. He solicited at the court of Augustus to be preferred to a greater ship whose commander had been killed. But without consideration it was given to another youth, the son of Libertina who waited on one of emperor's mistress. Gulliver called up Agrippa who was admiral in that fight. Agrippa confirms the whole account.

As one by one every person called up makes appearance, Gulliver is given to the melancholy reflection as to how much the human race has degenerated within these hundred years. The countenance has changed, the size has shortened, the nerves are unbraced, the complexion has grown sallow and the flesh is rendered loose. Gulliver cannot remain unmoved after comparing the living with the dead when he considers how these pure native virtues have been prostituted for a piece of money by their grandchildren, who in selling their votes and managing at elections have acquired every vice and corruption that can possibly be learnt in a court.

Critical Comments

In this Chapter, Gulliver continues his stay in Glubbduldrib, the land of magicians. The satire on history continues. The spirit of a philosopher points out that fashions of new systems come and go. Probably, there is a reference to Newtonian theories of science which Swift treated with contempt. There is also a satire also on how people turned into great historical figures by prostituting their wives and daughters, how history has glorified immoral persons and neglected virtuous people.

5

Gulliver comes back to Maldonada and after a fortnight's waiting, he sails to Luggnagg with two men. On the 21st April, 1709 they sail into the river of Clumegnig which is a seaport town, at the south-east point of Luggnagg. In Luggnagg, Gulliver is confined from the order of the court by the pilot on the ground of being a stranger. But he is treated kindly and further orders are awaited. The orders from the court are expected and Gulliver is produced on the appointed day and hour to lick the dust before the foot-stool of his Majesty. Two days after the arrival of Gulliver, he is commanded to crawl upon his belly and lick the floor as he advances. But as Gulliver is a stranger, care is taken that the floor is made clean and the dust is not offensive. When the king has a mind to put any of his nobles to death in a gentle manner, the king commands the floor to be sprinkled with poison. The noble licks it and dies in twenty-four hours. But the king is kind enough to get the floor wiped clean after every execution. At one time, a young man loses his life for the carelessness of the servant who maliciously neglects his duty to clean the floor. The king is kind enough to the servant and lets him off without punishment on the promise that he will not do so in future.

After crawling on his belly and licking the floor, Gulliver raises himself on his knees and then striking his head seven times on the ground pronounces the words as was taught him "May your celestial Majesty outlive the sun, eleven moons and a half." The king replies to Gulliver according to the custom. Then Gulliver speaks in his Balnibarbi tongue and his interpreter gives the meaning in that of Luggnagg. The king appoints a lodging for Gulliver in the court and arranges for his food and comfort. But Gulliver has a desire to come back to his wife and family.

Critical Comments

In this chapter, Gulliver visits Luggnagg where Gulliver has to lick lip the floor by crawling on his belly to meet the king. It is a satire on the way the king used to treat their subject by striping them completely of their human dignity. The cruelty of the king is also reflected in the event of sprinkling poisonous powder on the floor if the king wants kill anyone gently. Even the mistake of the servant who forgot to wipe the floor clean of poison and a man dies is pardonable as the justice and judgment of the king is final. It shows what happens when king turn arbitrary and whimsical.

6

The people in Luggnagg are polite and generous. Though they are not without some share of that pride which is peculiar to all eastern countries, yet they are courteous to strangers. One day Gulliver is asked whether he has seen any of their Struldbrugs or immortals. He expresses his desire to know about the immortals. He is told that sometimes a child happens to be born in a family with a red circular spot in the forehead, directly over the left eyebrow which is an infallible mark that it should never die. The spot is about the size of a silver three pence and gradually it grows larger. Gulliver considers Struldbrugs to be very fortunate for being immortal.

The Luggnaggians are desirous to know what the plans of Gulliver will be if he were immortal. His reply is that first he will make himself the wealthiest man in the kingdom. Then he will apply himself to the study of arts and science to excel all others in learning. Lastly, he will record every action and event of Princes, great ministers and other important persons and in this way he will be a living treasure of knowledge and certainly become the oracle of the nation.

Gulliver is informed that the Struldbrugs grow dejected and melancholy till they come to four score. There are not only opinionative, peevish, covetous, morose, vain, talkative and incapable of friendship and dead to all natural affections as Gulliver himself finds from personal observation. Envy and impotent desire are their prevailing passions. They are cut off from all possibilities of pleasure and whenever they see a funeral, they lament and rcpinc that others have gone to a harbour of rest to which they never can hope to arrive. They are despised and hated by all sorts of people, when one of them is born, it is reckoned ominous.

Seeing a number of immortals, Gulliver finds it the most horrifying sight that he has ever beheld. The women are more horrible than men. Besides, the usual deformities in extreme old age, they acquire an additional ghastliness in proportion to the number of years. Gulliver is ashamed of the pleasing visions he had formed and he rejects the desire to be immortal.

Critical Comments

This chapter is a satire on the human desire for immortality which Gulliver himself has for a time till he sees immortal human beings. Gulliver comes face to face with immortality in the form of Struldbrugs. Gulliver is disillusioned with immortality to see the immortal humans suffering from the infirmities of the old age and cursing their fate when they see somebody dead and feel they cannot get out of their helpless condition even by dying.

7

On the 6th May, 1709, Gulliver takes a solemn leave of his Majesty and all his friends. In six days, he finds a vessel ready to carry him to Japan and spend fifteen days in the voyage. They lead at a small port-town called Xamoschi situated on the south-east of Japan. At the custom-house, he shows the letter from the king of Luggnagg to his Imperial Majesty. On 9 June, 1709, he arrives at Nangasac after a very long and troublesome journey where he meets some Dutch sailors belonging to Amsterdam. He comes with them to Amsterdam and then sails to England. On 6 April, 1710, he puts in at the Downs. The next morning he lands in his native country after an absence of five years and six months. He goes straight to Redriff and finds his wife and family in good health.

Critical Comments

Here Swift winds up Gulliver's journey to Laputa. Here Gulliver departs from Luggnagg, comes to Japan and from Japan to England. The dates and circumstantial details lend an air of realism to the account of Gulliver's voyage. With this chapter one important phase of Gulliver's voyage comes to an end.

BOOK IV

A VOYAGE TO THE COUNTRY OF THE HOUYHNHNMS

1

After five months, Gulliver is offered the captainship of the ship, Adventure which he accepts happily. Gulliver with his crew is back to the sea on 7 August in 1710. Several of his men died of calenture. Gulliver is forced to recruit at Barbados and the Leeward island as he touched them on the way. But they turn out to be pirates and take Gulliver prisoner by binding him hand and foot on 9 May, 71 by rushing into his cabin. They leave Gulliver on the sea-shore of an unknown island after they have unchained him.

On this desolate island, Gulliver takes rest for a while and then goes up into the country resolving to meet savages who will be hostile to him. He walks very carefully for fear of being suddenly shot with an arrow from behind or either side. He is on the road where he sees many tracks of human feet, some of the cows and but most of the horses. Gulliver sees several animals in a field and one or two of the same kind sitting in the trees. Their shape is very singular and deformed. Their heads and breasts are covered with thick hair, some frizzled and lank. They have beards like goats and a long ridge of hair down their backs and fore-parts of their legs and feet but the rest of the body is bare. Their skins are of a brown buff colour. The females are not so large as males. They have long lank hair on their heads but none on their faces. The hair of both sexes is of several colours, brown, red, black and yellow. Gulliver has a strong feeling of antipathy to these animals. Full of contempt and aversion, he gets up and pursues the beaten road. Gulliver is spotted and attacked by these creatures. In the meantime, he is saved by a horse whose appearance makes them run away. Gulliver and the horse gaze at each other. Another horse appears and they greet each other in a formal way striking each other's right hoof. They go some paces off walking side by side like persons deliberating upon some affair of weight, often turning their eyes towards him as it were to watch that he may not escape. Gulliver is amazed at their action and behaviour.

When the discussion is over, the two horses come up close to Gulliver looking with great earnestness at his face and hands. The behaviour of these animals is orderly and rational that Gulliver cannot help thinking them magicians who have changed themselves into brutes with some particular purpose. Gulliver tells them his problem in his own language and seeks their help. When they listen to him they neigh frequently towards each other as if they are engaged in serious discussion. The first word which he can learn from them is "Yahoo." When they feel that he has learnt the word, they pronounce another word. "Houyhnhnms" which after some difficulty Gulliver can learn. The horses are amazed at his capacity. After some time, one of the horses leaves while the other makes him a sign to follow.

Critical Comments

As in Lilliput, Brobdingnag and Laputa, Swift in the country of the Houyhnhnms lands Gulliver in a brave new world where he encounters strange kinds of animals. The hairy animals have a human form and attack Gulliver for no reason. The horses or Houyhnhnms are amazingly rational and intelligent. As soon as they appear, the animals in the human form or the Yahoos who are attacking Gulliver move away from him. The Yahoos and the Houyhnhnms are the two symbolic counters with which Swift weaves the design of the fourth book.

Moreover, we continuously evidence as in other parts also the learning capacity of Gulliver. Wherever Gulliver goes he learns a new language.

2

After travelling about three miles, Gulliver and the Houyhnhnm (horse) come to a long kind of building made of timber stuck in the ground and wattled across. The roof is low and covered with straw. The Houyhnhnm makes Gulliver a sign to go in first. It is a large room with a smooth clay floor and a rack and manger extending to the whole length of one side. Beyond this room there are three others. Gulliver is led to the third room where after his entrance the mare soon rises from her mat and coming up close after having nicely observed him, gives him a most contemptuous look and repeats the word "Yahoo." But he is unable to understand why the mare is repeating the word "Yahoo."

Soon Gulliver is taken to the yard where the beast which Gulliver has already seen and Gulliver come close together. Their countenances are compared carefully by the master and the servant who are repeating the word "Yahoo" continuously. Gulliver is shocked to see the resemblance between the filthy beast whose name is Yahoo and himself.

The horse or Houyhnhnm offers Gulliver a root which he returns to him after smelling. Then he offers Gulliver a piece of ass's flesh from the Yahoo's kennel but he also returns it because it smells very offensively. The Houyhnhnm throws it to the Yahoo who devours it greedily. Then the Houyhnhnm shows Gulliver a wisp of hay and a fetlock full of oats, but he shakes his head to signify that neither of these is food for him. Then Gulliver sees a cow and expresses his desire to let him go and milk her. The Houyhnhnm leads back into the house and gives him a large bowl full of milk.

As there is nothing for Gulliver to eat, he thinks he can make bread of oats which may be sufficient to keep him alive with milk. He heats oats before fire and rubs off the husk. Then he beats them with two stones, takes water and makes them into a paste or cake to toast on the fire and eat them warm with milk. Sometimes he catches rabbits or birds by springer made of Yahoos' hairs and often gathers wholesome herbs which he boils or eats as salad. At first, he is at a great loss for want of salt but custom soon reconciles him to the want of it.

Critical Comments

Gulliver's description of the Yahoos is a highly effective device of satire to show how ridiculous humans are. Swift comments on human beings through the contrast between the Houyhnhnms and the Yahoos. The horses are clean and their diet is balanced and vegetarian. Though the Yahoos are human in form and features, they are filthy and stink and eat rotten meat and garbage. The physical similarity between Yahoos and human beings shocks and horrifies Gulliver. He is impressed with the Houyhnhnms and he badly feels that he is a Yahoo more than a Houyhnhnm. The inferiority of Yahoos to Houyhnhnms reflects that man is inferior to a horse. A horse or Houyhnhnm is superior because he is rational, sympathetic and not dangerous for anyone.

3

Everyone of the Houyhnhnm family including the master is desirous to teach Gulliver the language of the Houyhnhnm. A sorrel nag, a servant is employed for this purpose. Gulliver points to everything and enquires the name of it and writes down in his book and corrects his bad accent by desiring his family to pronounce it often. Their language approaches nearest to the High Dutch or German but is much more graceful and decent. The curiosity and impatience of his master Houyhnhnm are so great that he spends many hours to instruct him. The master is convinced that he is a Yahoo. But his learning ability, civility and cleanliness astonish him. He is also perplexed about his clothes. In about ten weeks' time he is able to understand most of the Houyhnhnm questions and in three months can give him some tolerable answers.

The word "Houyhnhnm" in their tongue signifies a horse which means the perfection of nature. Several horses and mares of quality come to visit him on the news that a wonderful Yahoo can speak like a Houyhnhnm. The

Houyhnhnms who come to visit him can hardly believe him to be a right Yahoo on account of his covering of the body with clothes. They are astonished to observe him without the usual hair on skin except on his head, face and hands.

One morning, when the master comes in his room, he is fast asleep, his clothes fallen off on one side and his shirt above his waist. The nag delivers in message to the master and he desires to see the covered part of his body. The Houyhnhnm is surprised to hear from Gulliver that nature teaches people to conceal some part of the body. The master Houyhnhnm looks around several times and comments that he is a perfect Yahoo. Gulliver expresses his uneasiness on being compared to the Yahoo, an odious animal for which he has extreme hatred and contempt. Gulliver begs he will forbear applying that word for him and pass the same order in his family and among his friends who come to visit him.

The master is curious to know about Gulliver's voyage and the race of the people Gulliver belongs to. Gulliver tells him that he has come from a very far country travelling upon the sea, in a great hollow vessel made of wood and larger than His Honour's house. He describes the ship to him in the best possible terms he can and explains by the help of his handkerchief displayed how it is driven by the wind. He tells him that upon a quarrel with the men on the ship he is set on this sea coast. Gulliver also informs him that in his country the human beings like himself are the only governing, rational animals and that in this country he is astonished to see Houyhnhnms act like rational beings. He also tells that he cannot account for the degenerated and brutal nature of the Yahoos who resemble in every part the human beings in his country.

Critical Comments

In this chapter, the satire on human beings continues as the comparison of Gulliver with Yahoos presents a contrast with the Houyhnhnms. The Houyhnhnms, like men, are rational but they do not quarrel. The Yahoos represent the human race while the Houyhnhnm represent the perfection of nature. Gulliver's attitude of misanthropy is taking shape at this point which goes on intensifying in the later chapters.

Gulliver shrinks from his comparison with the Yahoos so much that he begs the master to refrain himself from such comparisons and request his family and visitors to refrain from such remarks. This chapter also shows how quickly Gulliver learns their language.

4

Gulliver tells his master that if by good fortune he returns to his native land and relate his travels, everybody will believe he said the thing which was not. His countrymen will not consider it probable that a Houyhnhnm is the presiding creature of a nation and a Yahoo, the brute. Gulliver's master hears Gulliver's account with great signs of uneasiness on his face. He is unaware of such terms as doubting or not believing and does not know how to behave in such circumstances. He is ignorant of such expressions as "lying" "false representation." He feels great difficulty in what Gulliver means.

The Houyhnhnm asks Gulliver whether there is any Houyhnhnm in his country. Gulliver tells him that the Houyhnhnms in his country graze in the field and in winter they are kept in houses. The (Yahoo) human servants are employed to rub their skin smooth, comb their manes, serve them with food and make their beds. Hearing this, the master Houyhnhnm remarks it means whatever reason the Yahoos may pretend to have, the Houyhnhnms are the masters of human beings. In the opinion of Gulliver, the horses in his country are most generous and comely animals. They have excellent swiftness and strength and are employed in travelling, racing and drawing chariots. When they die, their skin is stripped and sold.

At this description, the master becomes indignant at the thought of men riding a horse. By considering the frame of Gulliver's body, he opines that no creature of equal bulk is so ill-contrived for using reason in the common matters of life. He begins to find fault with Gulliver's physique, the flatness of his face, the prominence of his nose, his eyes placed directly in front so that he cannot look on either side without turning his face that he is not able to feed himself without lifting one of his forefeet to his mouth etc.

As the master is keenly desirous to know about Gulliver's story before he came to the Houyhnhnmland. He tells him that he was born in an island, called England which is governed by a queen. He is a surgeon that cures wounds. He tells him how he was a captain of a ship in the last voyage and he was set on the seacoast by pirates. Gulliver tells the master horse his countrymen are forced to migrate from their country on account of poverty or crimes like robbery, forgery, rape or sodomy. Many spend their money in drinking, whoring and gaming. The master is shocked to know the vices of Gulliver's country and unable to comprehend why people practise such vices. Gulliver explains that all the evils are the result of the lust for power, riches, sex, malice. There are no words in the Houyhnhnm language for these vices. So Gulliver has to define all of them. There are no words also for power, government, war, law, punishment in their language. But as he has an excellent understanding, he comes to acquire a complete knowledge of what human nature in his part of the world is capable to perform especially in Europe and England.

Critical Comments

This chapter is a satire not only on the European society but the entire mankind. Swift here employs the technique of ironical reversal. Mankind is contrasted with the horses. Here horses are in the ruling position and men (Yahoos) are their servants. The chapter throws light both on the physical and mental defects of mankind. Man runs after power and wealth which are the chief reasons for corruption and evils. He indulges in war crimes, frauds and murder and these vices are not found in the dictionary of the horses or Houyhnhnms and this is why it is difficult for the master Houyhnhnm to understand them. The ironical reversal indicates that man proud of being rational animal is quite irrational in his behaviour and inferior to the noble horses of the Houyhnhnmland. The Yahoo, the symbol of the degenerate man seems to present the image of man.

5

Gulliver's master is more desirous to know about the state of England. Gulliver tries to give him the full account of Europe. Gulliver relates the revolution under the prince of

Orange. The long war with France started by this prince which continues even in the reign of the present queen in which a million Yahoos have lost their life, a hundred or more cities have been taken and many ships have been burnt or sunk.

The master asks Gulliver what are the causes and motives that make one country go to war with another. Gulliver answers that the causes are innumerable but he mentions a few. He says that sometimes the ambition of princes who never think that they have land and people enough to govern leads to war. Sometimes the minister engaged in corruption needs to divert attention of the subject against their evil administration. Sometimes one prince attacks another for fear of being attacked. Sometimes the war is there just because the enemy is very strong. It is a very justifiable cause of war to invade a country after the people have been ruined by famine, destroyed by pestilence or embroiled by factions among themselves.

Gulliver's master wants to know of 'law' because he is unable to understand that the law is intended for every man's preservation should not be any man's ruin. There is "a society of men who are trained up from their youth in the art of proving by words multiplied for the purpose that what is black is white according as they are paid. Thus lawyers enjoy full freedom to prove that the right is wrong and the wrong is right. As the lawyers are quite accustomed to defending falsehood, they have difficulty when they are advocates for justice. Moreover, they can be easily purchased by the enemy with more money. The men who are parties can be represented by lawyers only. They can plead their own case. The judges who are appointed to decide civil and criminal cases are chosen from among the lawyers. Having been biased all their life against truth and equity, they refuse even a large sum from the side justice lies. Thus they are "avowed enemies to pervert the general reason of mankind in every other subject of discourse as in that of their own profession."

Critical Comments

This chapter consists mainly of the descriptions of the European society. The picture painted by Gulliver of Europe or the civilized human society is horrible, particularly for the reasons stated for war and the way justice is dispensed in the society by the lawyers especially trained for this purpose. The greed of man, his irresponsible and immoral use of force are the causes of destructive wars in which millions of people are killed. The objects of satires are princes and kings whose greed knows no bounds and brings about wars. The second object is the profession of the lawyer which can be defined as the art of proving that right is wrong and wrong is right. The judges are selected from among them and the entire judicial system works to reward the criminals and deprive the people of their human rights. The picture of the civilized society of Europe as presented by Gulliver seems to be an honest account of things as they happen and the very statement of facts go against the kings and princes and the team of lawyers.

6

Gulliver continues to describe the way of life in England. Gulliver explains the value of money and the value of metals and coins. The Yahoo who has the great stone of this substance is able to purchase whatever he wishes to have, for example, the finest clothes, the best house, large area of land, the most costly food and drink etc. He describes the difference between the rich and the poor. Gulliver informs the master that England produces more food than the English people can consume and earns a lot through trade and commerce. Most people are compelled to live by begging, robbing, stealing, gaming, lying, hectoring, whoring and similar corruptions.

Gulliver tells the master that people drink wine because it makes them merry, diverts all merry thoughts, begets wild, extravagant imagination, raises hopes, banishes fears till they sleep a profound sleep. But the drink makes them diseased and their life uncomfortable and short. The prostitute Yahoos acquire certain diseases which are transferred to all those who come in their contact. The diseases are communicated from generation to generation. The doctors who claim to cure the disease are more interested in money-making than curing this disease.

Gulliver describes a Chief Minister of State who is completely free from joy and grief, love and hatred, pity and anger. He has only a strong desire for wealth, power and titles. A person can rise to the position of a Chief Minister by various methods by using his wife, daughter and sister, by betraying, undermining his predecessors and by a furious zeal in public assembly against the corruption of the court. The Prince generally chooses a Chief Minister who is the most obsequeous and subservient to the will of his master. A minister tries to save his position by bribing the majority of the senate or the council.

Most of the Europeans marry for money. Men are bred from their childhood in idleness and luxury. It leads them to marry a woman of mean birth. These women are most unsuitable but they do not care for the sake of money.

Critical Comments

In this chapter, Gulliver describes the European style of living of ministers, politicians, physicians etc. Swift shows the craze for luxury that spoils men and lust for money is one of the greatest weaknesses which constitutes the main criterion for selection of wives. Doctors suffer from the same disease. They are much more interested in money making than curing people. The court is fully involved in corruption. The criterion for the selection for a Chief Minister is his submissiveness and he can save his position always by bribing. Swift reveals that corruption is rampant in Europe. It is the criticism of the European life which is not only confined to the eighteenth century but probably extends to the civilized human society for all times as no place is free from malice, lust for power, money, corruption. Swift, thus, transmutes the particular and the temporal into the timeless and universal.

7

Gulliver is impressed with many virtues of the Houyhnhnms which contrast with the corruption of human life. Now Gulliver begins to view the actions and passions of man in a very different light that he resolves never to be with human kind and to pass the rest of his life among those admirable Houyhnhnms. But his fate does not favour him.

After obtaining answer to all the questions, the master expresses his views on human beings. He accepts that there is no doubt that human beings have reason but they have made use of it but to aggravate national corruptions. Human beings have multiplied their original wants and spend their whole lives in vain endeavours to supply them. It is clear that Gulliver has neither the strength nor the agility of the common Yahoo nor their speed nor the ability to climb the trees.

In his view the institutions of government and law in Europe are the manifestations of gross defect in reason and by consequence in virtue because reason alone is sufficient to govern a rational creature. The Yahoos are known to hate each other because of the odiousness of their shapes which they can see in others but not in themselves. They are greedy. They fight with each other but seldom kill anyone for want of the instruments of death that man has invented.

The Yahoos are mad after certain shining stones which they try to collect more and more and hide them in the most safe places so that others may not take them away. He realizes this madness for shining stones proceeds from the principle of avarice which Gulliver has ascribed to mankind. He informs Gulliver that two Yahoos fight with each other for the possession of shining stones and a third one takes advantage and carries it away from both of them. He also says that one of the most odious habits of Yahoos is to devour everything that comes in their way whether herbs, roots, berries and rotten flesh of animals. The Yahoos are also fond of drinking the juice of a certain root which produces the same kind of effect on them as liquor produces on the Europeans.

The Houyhnhnm adds that in his country only Yahoos are subject to any disease. They are cured by the mixture of their own dung and urine forcibly put into their mouth. They are very nasty and dirty while other animals are clean. The male Yahoos fight with each other for a single female Yahoo. The Houyhnhnm master also describes how often a female Yahoo stands behind a bush and lures a male Yahoo to some convenient place where the male follows her. At this time, the female Yahoo gives out the most offensive smell. Gulliver realizes that the female Yahoos are no different from the women in Europe and feels that coquetry is common to all woman-kind.

Critical Comment

This chapter contains criticism on the habits of human beings. Swift draws parallels between the Yahoos and human beings to show the superiority of the Houyhnhnms to man. The Houyhnhnms are logical and reasonable and they do not run after worthless materials as human beings and Yahoos do. The materialistic concerns are common to both Yahoos and human beings. The Houyhnhnms are also free from disease. The avarice and greed and the quarrelsome tendencies of men and Yahoos distinguish them from the race of the Houyhnhnms. This chapter like other chapters of the Book IV brings out the rational superiority of the Houyhnhnms over man.

8

Gulliver compares the character of the Yahoos as described by the Houyhnhnm master with that of man. He thinks he can make further discoveries from his own observations and decides to go among the herds of the Yahoos. He finds that the Yahoos are the most unteachable of all animals, their capacity limited to carry burdens. They have a perverse restive disposition. They are cunning, malicious, treacherous and revengeful. They are strong and but cowardly, cruel and insolent.

One day, Gulliver strips himself stark naked and goes into a river for bath. A young female Yahoo standing behind the bank sees the whole proceeding and gets inflamed by the desire. She jumps into the river and embraces him. Gulliver gets terribly frightened and roars as hard as he can. Then he is saved by his friend the sorrel nag. Now the master is fully convinced that Gulliver is a real Yahoo. This is why the female has a natural impulse to have him as of her own species.

On the other hand, Gulliver feels that the Houyhnhnms are endowed by nature with a general disposition to all virtues. They govern themselves wholly by reason and they have no idea of evil in a rational creation. Reason is never problematical with them as with human beings where men can argue with plausibility on both sides of the question. The two principal virtues among the Houyhnhnms are friendship and benevolence. There are not confined to particular objects but universally extend to the whole race. Even a stranger from the remotest place is treated as a neighbour. They preserve decency and civility to the highest degree.

The one chief quality of the Houyhnhnm is that the Houyhnhnms are cautious to prevent their country from being overcrowded. This is why after having produced one, sex, the female Houyhnhnm stops having sexual connection with her consort. The Houyhnhnms are extremely careful in selecting their brides. They choose such colours as will not make any disagreeable mixture in the breed. Strength is chiefly valued in the male and comeliness in the female to preserve the race from degenerating. There is no room for courtship, love, presents, jointures and settlement. The violation of marriage and unchastity is never heard of and the married couple pass their lives with the same friendship and mutual benevolence that they bear to all others.

In educating the youth of both sexes their method is highly desirable. Temperance, industry and cleanliness are the lessons equally imparted to both the sexes. The master Houyhnhnm considers it monstrous in men to give the females a different kind of education from the males except in some articles of domestic management. The Houyhnhnms train up their children to strength, speed and hardiness by exercising them in running up and down hills over hard stony grounds. Four times a year youths from different areas gather to exhibit their proficiency in running, leaping and other feats of strength and agility where the winner is awarded with a song made in her or his praise.

Every fourth year the meeting of the representative council of the whole nation is held for five or six days. Here the state and condition of several districts is enquired whether there is any shortage or excess of hay or oats or cows or Yahoos. If there is any wants, it is immediately supplied by unanimous consent and contribution.

Critical Comments

This chapter exhibits the contrast between the life and habits of the Yahoos and the life and habits of the Houyhnhnms. The Yahoos are described as the most filthy and noisy creatures as "the odious vermin," which has also been referred to in Book II chapter 6. This phrase links up the Yahoos with the human race which is "cunning," malicious treacherous, revengeful and cruel. The lustful nature of the female Yahoos has been specially emphasized to exhibit the lustfulness of the European women of the eighteenth century. On the other hand, the virtues of the Houyhnhnms stand as model for Gulliver. They attach great importance to reason and their reason is not problematical. Their love and affection is equal for everyone whether they are life-partners or strangers. The Houyhnhnms are careful to control the population and so they restrain themselves in intercourse. They are not lustful as the Yahoos. Gulliver is impressed with the decency of their life-style and concludes that they are endowed with all virtues of nature. It should be borne in mind that it is Gulliver not Swift who takes the Houyhnhnms as models for human beings because Swift himself believes that man cannot live by lopping off his desires and being absolutely rational.

9

A grand assembly is held in the Houyhnhnmland about three months before his departure. The debate is on the question whether the Yahoos should be exterminated from the face of the earth on the ground of being the most filthy noisy and deformed animal which nature has produced. They are also the most restive and steal the milk of their cows, kill and devour their cats and trample down their oats and grass. Almost all favour the idea that the Yahoos must be exterminated but Gulliver's master puts forward the view that they must not be exterminated. He says that instead of extermination of the Yahoos they should castrate the Yahoos when they are young in order to render them incapable of producing their species. Thus the whole race of the Yahoos will come to amend in the course of time without any destruction of life. He also suggests that they should cultivate the breed of asses who will be more useful than other animals.

The Houyhnhnms have no letters and consequently their all knowledge is traditional. They are subject to no disease and therefore they need no physicians. But they have excellent medicines composed of herbs to cure accidental bruises and cuts in any part of the body. They calculate the year by the revolution of the sun and the moon but use no sub-divisions into weeks. They are well acquainted with the notion of the sun and the moon and understand the nature of eclipses which reflects the great progress of their astronomy.

They are excellent in poetry. The aptness of their similes and the minuteness of as well as the exactness of their description are inimitable. The theme of their poetry is mainly friendship and benevolence or the praise of winners in races and other exercises.

Though their buildings are rude and simple, they are not inconvenient. They are well contrived to protect them from the effect of cold and heat.

The Houyhnhnms die only of old age and are buried in obscure places. At their death, their friends express neither joy nor grief nor does the dying person express the last regret that his life is coming to an end. They generally live to seventy or seventy-five years. Some weeks before their death they face a gradual decay but without pain.

Gulliver finds that they have no words to express evil except the ones that they acquire from the Yahoos. Then they denote the folly of a servant, an omission of a child, a stone that cuts their feet, unseasonal weather by adding to each the epithet of "Yahoo."

Critical Comments

This chapter like the previous is in the series of chapters which emphasize the contrast between the Houyhnhnms and the Yahoos. The Yahoos are so nasty, evil and harmful to the world that the Houyhnhnms are compelled to hold an assembly to debate the question as to how they should be exterminated. Later, the suggestion is accepted that instead of extermination they should be castrated. The Yahoos somehow represent the degenerate man and quite naturally, symbolically the question is raised as to how to obliterate the evils of man.

In contrast, the Houyhnhnms are represented as noble creatures as there is no word in their language for evils like lying or falsehood. They represent the virtues of the superhuman life, the perfection of rationality that the human beings can never attain. Probably this is why George Orwell finds them emotionally dead. They know no passions, no love, no enmity, rivalry, hope and despair except hatred for the Yahoo like the Jews in the Nazi Germany. It may be said that the creatures of Swift's imagination, the Houyhnhnms parallel the modern scientific creature known as robot who acts but is completely without human feelings and imagination. Quite naturally, the Houyhnhnms can never constitute ideal models for man. They represent unhuman rational perfection.

10

Gulliver lives happily among the Houyhnhnms. He has been given a small room which he plasters with clay and covers with rush-mat of his own contriving. There he enjoys perfect health of body and tranquillity of the mind. He feels free from the feeling of fear, treachery or inconstancy of a friend or the enmity of man. He has no occasion for bribing, flattering or pining to procure the favour of any great man. He needs no fence against fraud or oppression, in short no fear that a man has from another man. There are neither physicians to destroy his body nor lawyers to ruin his fortune.

Gulliver has the favour of being admitted to the presence of several Houyhnhnms who come to visit or dine with his master. They have a notion that when people meet, a short silence does much to improve conversation. During these intermissions, new ideas may arise. Their subjects of conversation are friendship and benevolence, order and economy, operation of nature and tradition or upon unerring rules of reason. Gulliver confesses that all the little knowledge he has of any value has been acquired from the lectures of his master and his friends. Gulliver appears impressed by the virtue and wisdom of the Houyhnhnm. He admires their strength, comeliness, speed and their constellation of virtues. He loses the attitude of awe that the Yahoos and other animals bear towards them. He has a blend of love and gratitude for them and hopes they will condescend to distinguish him from the rest of his species.

When he thinks of his family friend, his countrymen or human race, he considers them as Yahoos in shape and disposition except that their human counterparts are little more civilized and qualified with the gift of speech. They use their reason only to improve and multiply the vices of the Yahoos. Gulliver is so much impressed with the Houyhnhnms that he begins to imitate their gait. He trots like horses. Thus he considers himself a Houyhnhnm superior to the human species. When he looks at the reflection of his own face in a lake or fountain, he turns his face away in horror and detestation. Gulliver feels fully settled there for life. But one day he is shocked to hear from his master that at the last assembly of the Houyhnhnms it has been decided that Gulliver should not be allowed to stay in the Houyhnhnmland as he is a Yahoo. Gulliver should swim back to his own country. Hearing this, Gulliver falls in a swoon. When Gulliver comes back to his senses, he remarks that death is preferable to banishment from this land. Gulliver asks for two months' time for preparation and orders are passed to the sorrel nag to help Gulliver.

Gulliver is sad to depart from his master and desires to kiss his master's hoof. This master does him the honour of raising it gently to his mouth. Gulliver's eyes were overflowing with tears. He sits in the canoe which is made in two months' time and sets out on the sea.

Critical Comments

This chapter deals with the overimpressionability of Gulliver and this confusion in his mind that he is a Houyhnhnm. He is charmed by the superhuman virtues of the Houyhnhnms and repelled by the Yahoo and human way of living so much so that he has no desire to come back to the human world. Gulliver's misanthropy is confirmed by the effect of horror that he gets from the reflection of his own face in the lake of fountain. The irony is that Gulliver is broken-hearted at the time of his final parting from his master, his master is completely unaffected by this event. Gulliver is here the victim of irony when he has a desire to kiss the hoof of his master and he does him the honour of raising his hoof to his mouth. Swift is not only bitter in his satire as is supposed but comic also. The scene of Gulliver's departure is a case in point.

11

On 15 February, 1714-15 at 9 o'clock in the morning, Gulliver sets out for his voyage in his small boat. His master and his friends stand on the shore till he is out of sight. Gulliver often hears the gentle voice of the sorrel nag, "take care of thyself, gentle Yahoo."

Gulliver intends to discover some small island uninhabited because in his view it is a greater happiness than to be the first minister in the most polite court of Europe. Gulliver feels it horrible to live in the society under the government of the Yahoos.

On the fourth day, Gulliver reaches a small island where he sees stark naked men, women and children round a fire. They attack Gulliver but he succeeds in getting into his canoe and sails off. They discharge an arrow before he gets far into the sea. It wounds him badly in his left knee. As he looks for a secure landing place, he sees a ship which picks him up from his canoe. The sailors on the ship question him in Portuguese and Gulliver replies in the same language but in the tone of the Houyhnhnms. It makes them laugh because his way of speaking resembles the neighing of a horse. At this, Gulliver trembles between fear and hatred when Gulliver hears them talking. He feels it as monstrous as if a dog or cow should speak in England or a Yahoo in the Houyhnhnmland.

These sailors treat Gulliver with great humanity and then Captain Pedrode Mendis also treats in the same way. He shows courtesy and generosity. Though Gulliver is amazed at his behaviour, he remains silent and sullen. During the voyage Gulliver tries to leap into the sea and swim for his life rather than to live among the Yahoos. But he is caught and chained to his cabin.

The ship reaches Lisbon on November 5 in 1715. Gulliver stays in Lisbon at the captain's house for a few weeks. On the 24th November, 1715, Gulliver leaves Lisbon for England and reaches the Downs on 5th December, 1715 and reaches his home at Rotherhith. His wife and family receive him with great surprise and joy. But Gulliver is filled with disgust and contempt at seeing them on his arrival; he feels horrified and falls into a swoon almost an hour. After passing five years with the Houyhnhnms, he is unable to bear the sight of the Yahoos, even his wife and children. It is also with great difficulty that he eats with his wife and children.

Gulliver buys two horses with his money. For the peace of his mind or the revival of his spirit, he likes to spend his time with horses. He regards them as his true friends. Gulliver begins to record his experience in the book after five years of his return to England, but he neither likes his family nor feels comfortable with them.

Critical Comments

This chapter registers Gulliver's strong hatred for mankind. He cannot bear the sight of human beings, even his wife and children. Gulliver feels happy and comfortable in the company of the Houyhnhnms about whom he says they live in great amity with him. Gulliver feels the Houyhnhnms are far more civilized and gentle. So he has still the desire to live with them. But the features of the Yahoo that he bears in his form and figure account for his banishment from the Houyhnhnmland. This chapter gives an account of Gulliver's journey homeward from the Houyhnhnmland and record his disgust and contempt for humanity. This negative feeling is so strong that he is unable to accept his family.

12

Gulliver says that he has given a faithful account of his travels for more than sixteen years. He says that his chief aim is to make people wiser, better and improve their minds by bad as well good examples of his experience which he has recorded in his book. He wishes that all travellers will record their experiences and events in their book based on honesty and truth.

Gulliver hopes that whoever reads the virtues of the Houyhnhnms will be ashamed of his own vices, while he considers himself as the reasoning, governing animal of his country. Gulliver writes for the noblest end to inform and instruct mankind over whom he can pretend superiority for the advantage he has secured by conversing so long among the most accomplished Houyhnhnms. He writes it without any view of profit or praise.

It is whispered to Gulliver that as a citizen of England he is bound to report the discoveries of new lands to the government of England because according to the law or the government whatever land is discovered by the subject belongs to the crown. But Gulliver believes that instead of conquering these new lands, the government should send a sufficient number of English people to learn from the inhabitants of the discovered lands the principles of honour, justice, truth temperance, public spirit, fortitude, chastity, friendship, benevolence and fidelity in order to civilize the Europeans.

Gulliver takes leave of his readers by saying that he is going to enjoy his own speculations in the little garden at Redriff and contemplate those excellent lessons of virtue which he has learnt among the Houyhnhnms and also to instruct the Yahoos of his own family. He has allowed his wife to sit with him at dinner even though the smell of the Yahoo continues to offend him. He can reconcile to the Yahookind (mankind) if they remain content with those vices and follies only which nature has given them. He is not the least provoked at the sight of a lawyer, a pickpocket, a fool, a politician, a gamester a whoremaster, a traitor and so on. But whenever he sees the lump of deformity and disease both in body and mind smitten with pride, it breaks all the measure of his patience. He is unable to comprehend how the vice of pride can tally to such an animal while the wise and virtuous Houyhnhnms who have all excellence that can adorn a rational animal have no name for this vice in their language. The Houyhnhnms who live under the government of reason are no more proud of the good qualities they possess than human beings who are the most irrational creatures.

Critical Comments

This is the concluding chapter of book IV as well as of *Gulliver's Travels.* Here Gulliver as the writer of this voyage literature convinces in that his account of the fantastic lands, people and events is only a faithful account of what he saw, heard and found during his actual voyage to these places. He assures the reader that he has neither exaggerated nor distorted the truth as he found it. He was impressed by the Houyhnhnms who were free from the vice of lying. Ever since he has vowed that he will never tell a lie and there is no lying or falsehood in the book. The aim of writing the book is also stated which is to inform and instruct without any view towards profit and praise.

Gulliver expresses his abhorrence of mankind so much so that he cannot endure the smell of the members of his own family. It is with great difficulty that he permits his wife to sit at dinner with him.

The staple motive behind the writing of the book has also been stated which the critics have missed while considering Swift as a misanthrope and a whole lot of controversy has arisen around this point. Swift states that he is reconciled to man as long as he is content with the vices and follies that nature has given him. Gulliver is not provoked at the sight of man with his natural vice and folly. But whenever he sees the lump of deformity both in mind and baby smitten with pride, it breaks all the measures of his patience. At this point, we can identify Gulliver with Swift. His principal motive in writing this satire is to smash the pride of man which finds expression in the thoughts of the contemporary philosophy and scientists of the time of Swift. They believed in the progressive rational perfection of mankind. But Swift, the Dean believed in the doctrine of the original sin, the fall of man after which it is only possible for the degenerate man to rise only with the grace of God not through the progressive perfection of rationality.

7

A Brief Synopsis of *Gulliver's Travels*

BOOK I

Lemuel Gulliver was the third of the five sons of a Nottinghamshire family. He studied medicine and practised it. But he was not successful as a medical practitioner. Earlier he had acted as a surgeon on two ships. So when the offer came from William Prichard, the master of the Antelope, he accepted it. They sailed from Bristol on 4 May, 1699 to the South sea. A storm suddenly springs up and the ship is driven by the wind. As it strikes against a rock, it is split and Gulliver swims up to an island. Being too tired, he falls asleep when he wakes up next morning, he finds himself tied down the ground by little strings. When he tries to free himself, he is attacked with arrows by men who are only six inches tall. He is given food, drink and sedative and put to sleep. In his sleep he is shifted to a castle big enough for him to crawl into.

Gulliver comes to know the island, called, Lilliput. He learns about their habits, customs state and society. When a great office falls vacant, the candidates have to show their skills in tight-rope dancing and whoever jumps highest without falling gets the post. The prizes awarded are red, blue and green ribbons. Flimnap, the treasurer is skilled in such arts. Reldresal, the Principal Secretary for Private affairs comes next. Very often the chief ministers are commanded to show their skill to convince the emperor that they have not lost the faculty. It is morals, not the merit, which is considered in principle as a criterion for appointment.

Except for cottagers and labourers, the Lilliputans have to pay for the education of their children's. Girls and boys both are sent to school and they are given education which prepares them for the life suitable to the rank of their parents. They bury their dead with their head downward believing that in eleven thousand moons when they rise again, the earth will turn upside down.

Gulliver comes in contact with Reldresal, the Principal Secretary for Private Affairs. He explains to him the political life of the people. The grandfather of the emperor had passed the orders that eggs should be broken at the small end only. This made those furious who broke the eggs at the big end. There was a civil war. Eleven thousand people died in it. Volumes have been published on this controversy. The books of the Big-Endians have been prohibited and they are not considered fit for appointment. Many of the Big-Endians escape to a neighbouring island, called Blefuscu.

Gulliver is requested by the Emperor to capture the Blefuscu fleet. In spite of the shower of arrows, Gulliver captures fifty ships and brings them ashore. The Emperor confers upon him the highest honour by gracing him with the title of Nardac. Then the Emperor requests Gulliver to invade the kingdom of Blefuscu. Gulliver refuses to execute the idea and as a result there crops up an ill-will between Gulliver and the Emperor.

Once at the royal palace, the apartment of the emperor is on fire. There is a great hue and cry. Gulliver reaches the palace and extinguishes the fire by urinating on the burning portion of the palace. But the Empress has the great horror of what Gulliver has done and harbours a prejudice against Gulliver. She never gets her apartment repaired, never lives in that part of the palace and vows a revenge.

The ill-will grows and Gulliver is finally charged with treason. Gulliver is awarded death penalty. But the Emperor is kind enough to extenuate the capital punishment to the blinding of Gulliver. Gulliver escapes to the island of Blefuscu where he is treated well because he was instrumental in bringing about peace between the two kingdoms. The Emperor of Lilliput demands the return of Gulliver to undergo the sentence. But Gulliver finds a boat and sets out on the sea. He comes across a merchant ship of England. Gulliver gives the captain an account of his adventure. The captain thinks he is mad till he produces Lilliputian cattle and other things from his pockets. He reaches England safely.

BOOK II

Gulliver remains at home for two months. On 20 June, 1702, he is on the sea again for the East Indies. The ship is caught in a sea-storm and cast off in a different direction. When the storm is over, an island is sighted. The captain sends a few men in a boat to bring water. Gulliver accompanies them to see the land. There is nothing interesting around. Gulliver turns back to find that his fellow men in a boat are followed by a huge creature. Gulliver hides himself in the field of wheat for fear of being trampled. Gulliver is discovered when six of the giants enter the field for harvest. He is caught and carried by one of them to the owner of the field. The giant size people here are sixty-foot high and the grass and other things are equally large in size. The first night that he spends at the farmer's house, he is attacked by two rats of the size of the dog. Gulliver kills one and wounds the other. The island is called Brobdingnag.

The nine-year old daughter of the farmer, Glumdalclitch takes charge of Gulliver. He is called Grildrig. He easily learns their language and becomes quite friendly with them. The farmer puts Gulliver in the nearby city on the market day. Large crowds gather and pay their fees to see Gulliver. He is ordered by the royal court to be exhibited to the queen. On seeing the pranks of Gulliver, the Queen buys Gulliver from the farmer and he becomes part of the royal possession. The maids of honour often strip him naked from top to toe and put him full length against their bosom. Gulliver is disgusted with the smell of their body. A playful girl of sixteen set him astride on one of her nipples and plays with him.

Gulliver gives to the king an account of the life in Europe and his adventures on the sea. The king was not impressed by his account of the House of Lords and the House of the Commons in England. He does not understand why people are eager to enter the parliament. He wonders why a vulgar man can score a victory over better men by influencing his voters through money in election. When Gulliver informs the king that there are thousands of works on the part of government, he forms a very low opinion of Gulliver's countrymen because the king needs no endless discussion but common sense, reason and a sense of fairness and capacity of quick action. According to the king, whoever makes two ears of corns or two blades of grass grow where only one grew before did greater service to the country than all the politicians put together. Gulliver proudly tells the king about the invention of gun powder as one of the great achievements of man and the destructive uses to which it can be put. The king forbids Gulliver to mention such things before him again. His conclusion about man is that man is "the most pernicious vermin that nature ever suffered the crawl upon the surface of the earth."

But Gulliver personally wins the favour of the King and the Queen and travels with them to the sea-shore in a box. One day when they go about the sea, Gulliver asks his box to be placed near the sea in order to see the sea-shore. All of a sudden Gulliver finds his box rising and carried away by a giant eagle. The box is dropped on the sea where he is rescued by some English sailors and brought to England.

BOOK III

Lemuel Gulliver stayed ten days at home. Then comes the invitation from Captain Robinson to be the surgeon to his ship on a voyage to the East Indies in the north. They set out on the 5th of August, 1707. But soon they are set upon by pirates and tied down with ropes. One of the pirates is a Dutchman. Gulliver requests him to be kind to them. But instead of being released, Gulliver is put on a canoe with provisions for a few days. After five days, Gulliver reaches a rocky island where he sees a flying island which is lowered for him. Gulliver is drawn up by means of pulley. The flying island is called Laputa. The Laputans were a set of strange people with their heads cocked up in a particular direction and one eye turned inward and the other towards the zenith. The Laputans keep an island in complete subjugation. If the people over there rebel, they are punished with stones being dropped on them or the flying island being lowered to crush them to death. But this course is generally not adopted for fear that if lowered too much, the flying island may not rise again. The Laputans are all the time absorbed in thought and keep flappers and servants to remind them to use their particular sense, to see and hear. They are interested in mathematics. But when the clothes of Gulliver are prepared after taking his scientific measurement, the clothes hang loose on his body because the tailor makes a mistake in calculation. They are interested in music but they only hear the music of the spheres.

On his request to the king, Gulliver is sent to Lagado, the capital of Balnibarbi. It lies in ruins because a set of impractical projectors have visited it. They are engaged in projects which bear no fruit and neglect practical matters of life. The houses are clumsy, the fields without crops and everything is similarly neglected. They are dexterous enough in the management of the rule, the pencil and the divider but they have contempt for practical geometry and other branches of knowledge with the result that they fail in matters of practical life.

Gulliver also visits the Academy of Lagado where the professors or projectors are proud of discussing and always being engaged in useless, impractical experiments like extracting sunlight from cucumber, converting stool back into food and numberless experiments on flies and maggots. It is on account of their disregard for traditional wisdom and interest in innovations that the houses are clumsy, roads, in bad shape and agriculture, completely ruined. Lord Munodi is a successful land owner in Balnibarbi because he is a traditionalist and not interested in impossible innovations. The projectors or professors are engaged in the experiment of building a house from the roof and then moving downward and finding a device for one man doing the work of ten men and similar objects.

Gulliver also visits the island of sorcerers and magicians, Glubbdubdrib who can recall the spirits who die for twenty-four hours. Gulliver also goes to Luggnagg which is inhabited by people who are immortal. Gulliver is excited at the idea of immortality but to his disappointment they are suffering from old age infirmities and are lying in a helpless and hopeless condition. The king of Luggnagg gives a letter to the Emperor of Japan. In this way, Gulliver finds his way to a Dutch ship which brings him home.

BOOK IV

Gulliver is on the sea again when he is offered captaincy of a ship. At Barbados islands in the West Indies, Gulliver recruits seamen in order to replace men who died of tropical fever. They turn out to be pirates who put Gulliver on a boat and leave him on the mercy of winds and the sea. He reaches an island which is the strangest one that he ever came across. It is inhabited by noble horsemen or the Houyhnhnms and their servants, the Yahoos who have the human form. They have thick hair on their head and parts of their body. Gulliver's way is blocked by a number of such animals. Houyhnhnm appears on the scene. He directs the Yahoos to follow him. The Houyhnhnm treats Gulliver well, gives him food and shelter. Gulliver learns the language of the Houyhnhnms.

The Houyhnhnms are perfectly rational without being disturbed by irrational passions which are associated with the Yahoos. Gulliver gives the Houyhnhnm master an account of the life in England and Europe. As they are not wicked, they fail to understand the life of the people in England and Europe and Gulliver has to define the terms he uses in order to make them understand. Gulliver defines lying and the profession of the lawyers etc. Gulliver describes wars in Europe in which millions of people lost their life. The main cause of war is the ambition of princes who think that the land or people is not enough. There are also religious and ideological wars. The Houyhnhnm master tells Gulliver that the Yahoos hate each other. They could hurt each other with tooth and nail. They seldom kill each other for want of instruments of war that the Europeans possess.

One day, Gulliver takes off clothes for a bath in the river when a female Yahoo inflamed with passion follows him into the water. The way she embraces Gulliver, he is almost crushed. Gulliver is disgusted with the giant-size she-Yahoo's behaviour and dislikes the smell of her body at that time. The female Yahoos there used to let the male Yahoos to pursue her. She will hide herself in a place where the male

Yahoo can discover her easily. The Yahoos have great love for yellow metal which they collect and hide.

Gulliver is attracted to the perfectly rational life of the Houyhnhnms who know no friend, no love except benevolence. Gulliver identifies Yahoos with mankind and wants to stay on there. But the legislative assembly of the Houyhnhnms declares that Gulliver is a Yahoo and therefore he should live with the Yahoos or go back with a little sadness. Gulliver parts from his Houyhnhnm master, boards a Portuguese ship and reaches back home. He has not got over his hatred of the Yahoos and mankind and prefers horses.

8

The Significance of the Four Voyages

BOOK I

Gulliver's Travels is a scathing satire on mankind. The satire is delivered in terms of irony. The first voyage of Gulliver lands him in Lilliput where people are six inches tall and their houses and other things are accordingly small. They are like toys or dolls to Gulliver. But the little doll-like men act exactly as the full-size men do. They represent the English life in the time of Swift as well as a satirical microcosm of mankind. Thus the first book of *Gulliver's Travels* throws ironical light on "the smallness of the means, the vanity of the motives, the illusion of catchwords, through which kings retain their thrones and magistrate their office and from one end of the society to other the fearful influence of man upon man is exercised." In this connection, the language in which the six inch tall emperor of Lilliput is addressed is remarkable.

"Golbasto Momaren Evlame Gurdilo Shefin Mully Ully mighty Emperor of Lilliput, delight and terror of the universes whose dominions extend five thousand blustrugs (about twelve miles in circumference) to the extremities of the globe; monarch of all monarchs, taller than the sons of men; whose feet press down to the centre, and whose head strikes against the sun; at whose nod the princes of the earth shake their knees; pleasant as the spring, comfortable as the summer, fruitful as autumn dreadful as winter."

The irony is obvious. It is not only the dissection of the English political life of his time only but the monarchy itself and the paraphernalia that surround it.

Though in choosing persons of all employments, they have more regard to good morals than to great abilities, when an important position falls vacant, the candidates have to perform tight-rope dancing or with the badges of favour by leaping over sticks and creeping under them. Sometimes the ministers too have to act in the same fashion to show they have not lost the faculty to please the emperor. These childlike games imply that courtiers are rewarded only when they perform like clown at the beck and call of the emperor. The red, green and blue ribbons with which the courtiers are rewarded represent also the awards instituted by Queen Anne in 1703, by George I in 1725 and the one bestowed upon Walpole in 1726 respectively.

The conflict between Big-Endians and Small-Endians or the High-Heeled and the Low-Heeled represents the religious wars between Catholic France and Protestant England as well as the petty politics in which the political parties engage themselves as the whole quarrel is about how to break the eggs. Lilliput and Blefuscu are England and France and the two parties represent the Whigs and Tories.

The Empress who harbours a prejudice against Gulliver after his extinguishing the fire in her apartment by urination is Queen Anne who after the publication of *A Tale of Tub* was suspicious of Swift and never considered him fit to hold the position of a bishop and he had to remain content with deanery of St. Patrick's in Dublin. Bolgolam represents the Earl of Nottingham who used his influence to block Swift's promotion. Flimnap, the Lord Treasurer of Lilliput is Sir Robert Walpole who displayed his skill in the art of Parliamentary and political intrigues. There is a close parallel between Gulliver and Lord Bolingbroke. Like Gulliver, he brought a great war to an end between England and France. Like Gulliver, he was condemned by his political opponents for not bringing about the complete surrender of the enemy and accused of culpable association with French ambassadors.

Lemuel Gulliver's voyage to Lilliput is full of topical allusions to the contemporary England, but they are transmuted into the symbolic allegorical caricature of the institutions of mankind and provides a mirror to man with all his smallness and pettiness.

BOOK II

Swift transposes the scale in Gulliver's voyage to Brobdingnag. While in Lilliput, Gulliver was among the little dolls, in Brobdingnag where people are sixty-foot tall, Gulliver is himself like a doll among the giants and the rest is adjusted on the same scale. The former was the parody of the human reality which the custom invests with grandeur, in the latter, the human reality reveals itself as ridiculous and infinitely small.

Gulliver calls Lilliputians "small men" as they are not only physically small but their size represents their moral size. The giants of Brobdingnag treat Gulliver like a small dangerous animal or insect or a doll. Gulliver finds that the giants are kind and decent, though the farmer who catches him in the field makes lots of money by exhibiting Gulliver in the fair. It shows giants are not all perfect. Some are greedy as well. Swift concentrates on the superiority of the giants and the insignificance of Gulliver. He is only aware of his disadvantage on account of being a pigmy before the giants. He is not only threatened by monkeys and dogs but he is humiliated by maids as they treat him as a doll and strip him from time to time. Gulliver gives the king an account of the customs and traditions of England. But the pride of Gulliver is shattered by the remarks of the king of Brobdingnag. "While colour came and went several times, with indignation, to hear our noble country, the mistress of arts and arms, the scourge of France, the arbitress of Europe, the seat of virtue, piety and honours, and truth, the pride and envy of the world so contemptuously treated." He had a very low opinion of English or human civilization. Gulliver records the fact that, "I remember very well, in a discourse one day with the king, when I happened to say there were several thousand books among us written upon the art of government, it gave him directly contrary to my intentions a mean opinion of our understanding. He professed both to abominate and despise all mysteries, refinement and intrigue either in a prince or minister, he could not feel what I meant by secrets of state where an enemy of some rival nation were not in the case." He thought common sense and reason, the ability to do justice, levity and speedy determination of civil and criminal courses were only necessary for the king. He held the notion that "whatever could make two ears of corn or two blades of grass to grow upon a spot of ground where only one grew before would deserve better of mankind and did more essential service to his country than the whole race of politicians put together." Gulliver is proud of the inventions of gunpowder as one of the great achievements of man and the destructive uses to which it can be put. The king forbids him to mention such obnoxious things again in his presence. The moral superiority and the intellectual clarity of the king of Brobdingnag is far superior to those of Gulliver. Gulliver's pride is a common failing of man which needs to be humbled. The king rightly observes the history of Gulliver's country is one of frauds and deceits. He tells Gulliver that the English should be compared to the Lilliputians and thus tells him indirectly that he has committed the folly of comparing himself with moral giants.

There are few contemporary allusions in Brobdingnag. It may be said that here the king is the mouthpiece of the Tory party as well as of Swift's views on politicians, his animosity to lawyers, his sympathy for the poor farmers in Ireland under the tyranny of English rulers and Tories' denunciation of the practice of mercenary army in the midst of peace among a free people find expression through the character of the king of Brobdingnag.

BOOK III

The third voyage of Gulliver takes him to Laputa, Balnibarbi and Struldbrug. Here Swift represents his opinion and that of the contemporary wits and scholars who found much of the work of the Royal Society intellectually contemptible. In the age given to burlesque and satire, scientists were derided for triviality, pedantry and lack of practical usefulness in their studies. The self-regarding seriousness seemed disproportionate to the mean and vulgar objects of some of their inquiries, "useless experiments on Flies Maggots, Eels in vinegar and the Blue as Shadwell described in his play "The Virtuoso." This was the attitude of Samuel Butler (*The Elephant and the Moon*), Addison and Steele and Dr. William King. It is just possible that the burlesques of Dr. William King provided the suggestions for Swift's Academy of Lagado in *Gulliver's Travels* where he expressed his disgust with many of the projects of the scientists. Swift had closely read many of the scientific writings of his day and the voyage to Laputa is full of contemporary allusions. The technological benefits of science were slow in appearing and it was Swift who summed up the general attitude about the apparent uselessness of scientific inquiry when he applauded the Brobdingnagians because their study of mathematics is "wholly applied to what may be useful in life to the improvement of Agriculture and all Mechanical Arts," as Gulliver comments. Swift's opinion of the scientific achievement of his day is in itself inadequate and considered an attack on science. The voyage to Laputa is unfair in its criticism. But as allegory on the frivolous attitude to life, it is inconsistent.

The voyage to Laputa, according to Kathleen Williams is not merely topical satire on the Royal Society but presents a political philosophy and a comment on man's relation to nature which go beyond the topical scientific discoveries or the relation of the kingdoms of England and Ireland. The flying island suggests the relation of the king and the country. Laputa is dependent on Balnibarbi as its motions are dependent on the magnetic quality of the king's dominions. This quality has determined and established the power of the king over the fixed island. But there is a reciprocal dependence between them because if either side presses its power too far, the result would be disaster. This is why the flying island is not lowered too much and the ministers who attend the court of Laputa have their estates on the continent below.

Moreover the relationship between the greater and lesser magnets of Laputa and Balnibarbi is a comment on the limited usefulness of the laws of the universe upon which the Newtonian era prided itself. It is clear from the fact that the scientists of Laputa cannot explain if the flying island is lowered far too much why it cannot rise again. On the other hand, in spite of all the ingenuity of the flying island, the Laputan King is dependent on the fixed earth below for every movement that it can make. Symbolically, it represents the fact that after all, the theoretical achievement of man, practically man is dependent on, and determined by other men and laws of nature which he can neither alter nor fully understand.

The physical features of Laputans express their nature "one of their Eyes turned inward and the other directly up to the zenith" because they have lost their human quality in their abnormal absorption in things remote from human concerns like the study of stars. Because of their disregard of the evidence of senses, the Laputans are "very bad reasoners." Gulliver's ill-fitting suit and the barren fields of Balnibarbi illustrate it. The Laputans with their absorption in music, mathematics and astronomy represent the members of the Royal Society and also those who think by turning away from the sensory impressions and human concerns they can reach eternal truth "Brobdingnag presents a contrast to Laputa, a simple utopia of abundance" where the government is conducted with goodwill and regard to traditional wisdom "making two ears of corn and two Blades of grass, to grow where only one grew before." Gulliver found Balnibarbi in a chaotic condition and could "not see one Ear of corn or Blade of Grass." The Laputans' experiments have failed to bear fruit as their aims are impossibly high and unrelated to real condition. Lord Munodi is a successful land owner in Balnibarbi because he is a traditionalist and is not interested in the impossible innovations. Marjorie Nicolson and Nora Mohler in 1937 in "The scientific Background of Swift's voyage to Laputa" and "Swift's Flying Island in the voyage to Laputa" *Annals of Sciences* discovered that Swift used *The Philosophical Transactions* and the publications of *The Royal Society* for all but two of the projects of Grand Academy. Swift does not trust the scientific knowledge of Bentley and Newton's theory of gravitation which was a prelude to the scientific quest of the world later on.

The Struldbrugs are wretched for their prospect of endless life. They curse their fate that they cannot bring an end to their endless suffering.

BOOK IV

It is the fourth book, "The Voyage to the Country of the Houyhnhnms" that Swift's satire rises to an intensity of pitch where Swift's intention "to vex the world" by writing *Gulliver's*

Travels is clear as daylight. It has also led to a controversy and the charge of misanthropy against Swift. That this part of the book is quite rich is clear from the fact that it has led critics to extract several and various interpretations from its texture.

Swift has adopted the technique of reversal in this book. The horses or the Houyhnhnms are noble and lead life according to laws of reason and nature, while the Yahoos, human in form, are brutes, filthy and stink and eat rotten meat and garbage. The Houyhnhnms are the masters of the Yahoos. Swift presses home the contrast between the Houyhnhnms and the Yahoos. Gulliver's house is mid-way between the Houyhnhnms and the Yahoos. Swift contrasts the natural innocence of the Houyhnhnms with the natural depravity of the European Yahoos. This is obvious from the fact that words like power, government, war law and punishment and lie are beyond the comprehension of the Houyhnhnms.

Swift manipulates the three elements, Gulliver, the Houyhnhnm and the Yahoo for his satiric effects. The central ironic device of the fourth voyage is literalisation, the reduction of the symbolic or mental to the physical. The reverse is also true. Gulliver finds savages (horses) noble and Yahoos savage. Man is equated with a totally irrational animal. Gulliver's account of the European and English life to the Houyhnhnm suggests that men use reason to cover up their excuse for wars and conflicts and invention of gun and lead a thoroughly debased and corrupt life.

Though Gulliver treats the Houyhnhnms as ideal creatures but as George Orwell points out they are emotionally dead. They are generally benevolent but are exempt from love, friendship, curiosity, fear, sorrow and except in their feelings towards the Yahoos, who occupy rather the same place in the community as the Jews in Nazi Germany—anger and hatred. "It is a dreary utopia." Although Gulliver has got the horror of the Yahoos and tries to imitate the Houyhnhnms in their speech, walk and manners, Gulliver is identified with the Yahoo by the Houyhnhnms and they reason that Gulliver is a more civilised Yahoo, he remains Yahoo, all the same and so he is advised to swim back to his native place.

Upto the twentieth century, the critics identified Gulliver with Swift and his views with Swift's and their natural conclusion was that Swift was a misanthrope in the IVth book. But the study of Swift's irony in the twentieth century has led to delink Gulliver from Swift because Gulliver himself is the victim of irony. Gulliver says that he "took second leave of my master but as I was going to prostrate myself to kiss his hoof, he did me the honour to raise it gently to my mouth." Similarly, after this his return home, he is horrified at the sight of his family. He trembles and cannot stand the smell or the sight of his Yahoo-like wife and children.

Though Gulliver is the ironic victim of Swift and cannot be identified with Swift, at times we feel the voice of Gulliver merges with the voice of Swift in the merciless dissection of the English or European human life in the fourth book. Swift did not believe in the progressive perfection of man through science and reason and many of the thinkers of his time envisaged. He was the Dean of St. Patrick's cathedral who believed in the original sin and the consequent fallen state of man without the grace of God. Therefore the pride that the contemporary thinkers associated with the rational and scientific achievement leading to the perfection of man is actually is debunked in the fourth voyage to the country of the Houyhnhnms. The Yahoo is the image of the fallen man who has lost the capacity to lead a decent life of reason. The aim of Swift is to demolish the pride of the Yahoo who cannot rise without the grace of God.

9

Gulliver's Travels as a Children's Classics

Jonathan Swift's *Gulliver's Travels* has been described as a children's classics. It is quite interesting as a tale of adventures like Lewis Carrol's *Alice in the Wonderland* or Daniel Defoe's *Robinson Crusoe.* It arouses the interest and curiosity of the children to follow the events for their strangeness and remoteness from the real world. Swift like Walter Dela Mare's *Martha* transports the children to the land of imagination which is sometimes inhabited by six-inch tall men and sometimes by sixty-foot tall men, sometimes by strange innovators, sometimes by reasonable horses and ignoble human beings.

The tale of voyages is quite diverting. The complete matter-of-fact account is reminiscent of Defoe. But *Gulliver's Travels* appears as a children's classics if we move on the literal surface of the book. The texture of the book is rich and complex. If we read between the lines, the children's classics turns out to be a bitter and comic satire on Englishmen and mankind in general. Gulliver serves as the looking glass for the reader and the writer who presents a satire on the contemporary England and on mankind. *Gulliver's Travels* is apparently a book of voyages and travels but is actually a running commentary on the nature and behaviour of mankind which is devastating in its effect. The diversity of interpretations and of views on the book reflects the rich complexity of the book as an achievement of high literary excellence.

From this viewpoint, *Gulliver's Travels* is no less interesting. The voyage of Gulliver to Lilliput introduces us to the wonderland where men are six-inch tall. Their houses, animals, trees and other things are accordingly tiny and small. The physically small people are not only small in body. They reflect in their various activities of life the smallness of man, his meanness, malice, ingratitude, hypocrisy, cruelty and flattery. Lilliput is a strange fantasy and symbolically England and her people.

Similarly, Gulliver's voyage to Brobdingnag introduces us to as strange a world as Lilliput itself. While in Lilliput people were like dolls to the gigantic size of Gulliver, now Gulliver is a doll by the gigantic figures of Brobdingnag. Gulliver is a pet animal for the nine-year old daughter of a farmer in Brobdingnag. Later, he is sold to the queen who is interested in possessing Gulliver as a freak of nature. The size of the sixty-foot Brobdingnagians reflects their largeness of heart and mind against the inhabitants of Lilliput, England, Europe and all mankind. They treat Gulliver like an insect and bring close to their eye in order to examine them. Gulliver is afraid of falling down from a height and being dashed to pieces. Their grass, trees, roads and houses were proportionately very big. Gulliver tells the king of Brobdingnag about the English and European people and their way of living. The king formed a very low opinion of the whole country of Gulliver. He despised all mystery, refinement and intrigue either in a prince or a minister. He could not understand what Gulliver meant by "the secrets of state where an enemy or a rival nation were not in the case." He confined the art of governing within very narrow bonds of the common sense, reason, justice, speedy resolution of civil and criminal cases. His opinion was that whoever was able to grow two ears of corn where one grew would deserve better of mankind and did more essential service to the country than the whole race of politicians put together. His final remark on the conspiracies, rebellions, murders, massacres, revolutions, banishments avarice, hypocricy, perfidious cruelty, rage, madness, hatred, envy, lust, malice or ambition is that the Englishmen were "the most pernicious race of odious little vermin that nature ever suffered the crawl upon the surface of the earth."

The third voyage to Laputa is equally strange where people cock their head towards the sky with one eye turned inward and another outward. The main occupation of the Laputans is to keep an island in complete subjugation. They fly their island over this island below, drop stones over the people below or lower the flying island to crush the people to death. But this is rarely done because after lowering once it is just possible that the flying island may not rise again. Gulliver visits Lagado, the capital of Balnibarbi. It is in ruins because it was visited by a bunch of impractical planners known as projectors like extracting sunlight from cucumbers. He also visits a nearby place called Glubbdubdrib, an island of sorcerers and magicians. The governor of this place could recall to earth for twenty-four hours anyone who had died. Then he goes to Luggnagg. Here he comes across people who are immortal who continued to live for ever. At first, Gulliver is enthusiastic about the prospect of living for ever. But he discovers that most people suffer from the infirmities of old age and continue to exist in a hopeless and helpless condition. The Laputans neglect practical matters to indulge in theory. Their houses are very ill-built, the wall without one right angle in the apartment. They are interested in mathematics and music and are complete strangers to "imagination, fancy and invention." Professors are engaged in discovering rules and methods of agriculture, building new tools for trades and manufacturers whereby one man shall do the work of ten and a palace may be built in a week to last for ever. The attack is on the scientific and philosophic speculation of his time.

The fourth book of Gulliver's travels is a satire on the Englishman and mankind in general. Gulliver's disgust of the human beings is so great that he turns into a comic character. The fourth voyage of Gulliver takes him to the country of the Houyhnhnms. The Houyhnhnms are a race of noble horses who live according to the laws of reason and nature. The Yahoos, the degenerate species of men serve them. Gulliver recognises the Yahoos as detestable but to his "horror and astonishment" those "abominable animals had perfect human figures." Gulliver becomes the humble admirer of the virtues of the Houyhnhnms. He gives an account of his country to the Houyhnhnms which proves that the defects of England were the results of "defects in reason, by consequence, in virtue." We hear the voice of Swift in Gulliver's: "Now your honour is to know that these judges are persons appointed to decide all controversies of property as well as for the trial of criminals and picked out from the most dexterous lawyers who are grown old or lazy and having been biased all their lives against truth and equity lie under such a fatal necessity of favouring fraud, perjury and oppression that I have known several of them to have preferred a large bribe from the side where injustice lay rather than injure the faculty, by doing anything unbecoming to their nature or their office. The entire system of the English people has been stripped of the film of familiarity. Gulliver has got an instinctive horror of the Yahoos and finds difficulty in adjusting with the English Yahoos or men in England after his experience with the noble Houyhnhnms.

10

THE STRUCTURE OF *GULLIVER'S TRAVELS*

Jonathan Swift's *Gulliver's Travels* is the "faithful History" of Gulliver's travels. The circumstantial details like Gulliver's letter to his cousin, Sympson complaining of errors in early editions, a portrait of the author and traveller, the maps locating Lilliput, Brobdingnag, Laputa and Houyhnhnmland, the dates of discovery and the factual style establish the veracity of the account. It might stand beside *Robinson Crusoe* as a classic of realism. But *Gulliver's Travels* is more complex and rich in texture and structure than *Robinson Crusoe* on account of utraquistic nature of the work.

The unity of the book or structure is to be sought in the voyages, their parallels and contrasts, the repetition of the central theme of the book in its depth and intensity in every subsequent voyage and its culmination in the fourth voyage to Houyhnhnmland. Though the voyages owe their existence to Gulliver's "insatiable Desire" of seeing foreign countries. His adventure in the "brave new world" in each voyage is preceded by a somewhat similar accident. His discovery of Lilliput occurs as his ship splits on a rock. He is left by fellow shipmates in search of water on the sea-shore of Brobdingnag when they are pursued by a Brobdingnagian. In the third voyage to Laputa, he is set adrift in a canoe by the pirates who ransack the ship. In the fourth voyage to Houyhnhnmland, the mutinous crew-turned pirates exile Gulliver in a deserted shore. So all his incursions into the fantastic world are the result of an unhappy accident. Thus the preceding circumstantial background prepares us for the incursions into the brave new world every time.

The four books are linked by contrast. Though the contrast

between the first two books is sharp and obvious, it is not so between the second and the third and the third and the fourth. Though it is generally found true that "the rogue never hazards a metaphor," yet as Middleton Murrey finds, metaphor is the mode of apprehension with Swift. The entire fiction explodes the myth of human pride which is an absurd vice. In the first two books, the symbolism is a matter of minification and magnification but in the last two books the abstract ideas take on concrete shape. The useful mathematics of Brobdingnag is contrasted with the impractical interests of Laputans. The clothes made by them for Gulliver by taking his altitude by a quadrant do not fit him. The desire of the inhabitants of Struldbrugs for immortality and their plight are in sharp contrast with the indifference of the Houyhnhnms to death. The accumulation of circumstantial detail is the datum for the dual perception for his ironic vision which sets it apart from a book like *Robinson Crusoe.*

Gulliver in Lilliput comes across a people who are six inches tall and their emperor tall just by the breadth of the nail. They are expert mathematicians. Their laws appear to be logical, natural and appealing. But the gap between the practice and the principle is wide. Their physical size represents their moral and intellectual size. They are the worst embodiments of pride, pettiness, malice, cruelty, and ingratitude under the guise of their opposites. The central theme of the book is the absurd pride of man and the four books are united by the theme, though they appear to be voyages to the completely different worlds altogether. The size of the inhabitants of the Brobdingnag is just the reverse of the Lilliputans. They are sixty-foot tall. Their physical height represents their moral and intellectual height. They are generous, hospitable and, thus, just the reverse of Lilliputians. Gulliver in Brobdingnag reads morality and history which shows how diminutive, contemptible and helpless an Animal was man in his own Nature, "excelled by one creature in strength, by another in speed, by a third in Foresight, by a fourth in industry." On hearing the account of the English, or European human world, the king of Brobdingnag concludes mankind to be a "most pernicious Race of Little Odious vermin that Nature ever suffered to crawl upon the surface of the earth." The irony consists in Gulliver's view of similar comments as the result of ignorance and narrow-mindedness.

The third book covers the voyage to Laputa, a flying island peopled by the inhabitants absorbed in abstract speculation and impractical projects. The entire book is based on the separation of the mind from the senses. Their mental concentration is so great that they have to keep flappers who flap on their eyes or ears or the senses they are reminded to use. The professors at their Academy are engaged in funny projects which have failed to yield fruits and destroyed 'agriculture or the things of help to man that existed earlier. Their houses are clumsy, hair shabby, fields, wastelands, clothes designed by tailors are oversize. In fact, they have scored total failures in practical affairs of life. It is a satire on the useless application to futile projects by the scientists of the day.

The fourth book is the voyage to the Houyhnhnmland which is the culmination of the three preceding books. In the voyage to Lilliput, the first book, the reader had to adjust himself to the size of man, only six inches tall and the rest would follow as a natural corollary. In the voyage to Brobdingnag, the second book, the minification of Lilliput is replaced by magnification as the men are sixty-foot tall. Once the reader accepts it, the rest follows quite naturally. In the third voyage to Laputa, the people with one eye turned inward and the other outward, the inhabitants reflect the consequences of overemphasizing only one faculty. But in the fourth book, the voyage to the Houyhnhnmland, our view of man is turned upside down. The surprise in store for us is of a completely different order. Gulliver comes across horses, Houyhnhnms and men-like creatures who serve them and are called Yahoos. To our surprise, the Houyhnhnms are quite noble and rational and the Yahoos who are like Gulliver in form are quite beastly.

The charge of misanthropy against Jonathan Swift is based on the fourth book of *Gulliver's Travels*. The horses or Houyhnhnms are so uncorrupt that they fail to conceive the idea of a lie which Gulliver defines as saying something that has not happened at all. Gulliver is distinguished from Swift as we consider the picture of Gulliver conversing with horses at his home. Gulliver considers the Houyhnhnms as "animal rational and the wisest people on earth." Houyhnhnm in their language means perfection of nature. They are invested with virtues of friendships, benevolence, rationality and devotion to duty and the Yahoos are attributed with corresponding vices. Gulliver identifies the Yahoo with man. Gulliver tried to become a member of the Houyhnhnm family. But the assembly of the Houyhnhnms recognises him as a Yahoo and he is exiled from his utopia to his own species because "in a civilized Man of Quality, the imperfections of his mind run parallel with those of his Body."

The charge of misanthropy against Swift lies in the failure of critics to distinguish between Gulliver and Swift. Utraquism is the characteristic feature of *Gulliver's Travels* which sets it apart from the rest of the voyage literature or travelogues like *Robin Cursoe.* Swift said in his earlier book, "Satire is a sort of Glass wherein Beholders do generally discover everybody's face but their own." But the fourth book of *Gulliver's Travels* forces this truth upon Gulliver that all Yahoos are of the race of man which results in his exile from his adopted Houyhnhnmland.

11

IRONY IN *GULLIVER'S TRAVELS*

Irony is a technical literary term. It implies a contrast between appearance and reality, an incongruity between two sets of words and phrases or between words and the situation. Hence there are two kinds of irony. The incongruity or contrast between two sets of words and phrases is described as verbal irony and the contrast or incongruity between words and the situation is described as the irony of situation. It is described in tragedy and comedy as dramatic irony where the speaker is aware of the surface meaning of words but the audience perceives its application on a deeper level as the audience knows more than the speaker or character on the stage. The verbal irony in Dryden's poetry takes the form of wit which results in the ridicule of the satiric victim. In Pope it leads to subtle satire which belittles the victim of satire. In Shakespeare it lends tragic depth and significance. In Swift, the irony of situation results in devastating effects.

Jonathan Swift is the master of irony, both verbal irony and the irony of situation. Irony is the staple vehicle of Jonathan Swift's viewpoint in his works, as Swift is acutely conscious of the gap between the ideal and the actual. Swift's vision is essentially ironic. Therefore irony is not just a technical device but the essential and integral part of Swift's outlook on life embodied in his works of art. The effect of irony in Swift is not Drydenian which results in the laughter of ridicule. Swift strips the world of the film of familiarity and then shows the absurdity of the English or human behaviour very innocently and the reader is immediately conscious of its application to the familiar world we inhabit. The satiric effect is achieved in terms of completely feigned innocence of the speaker which reveals the gap between the ideal and the actual. Swift developed this art from the very beginning and perfected it in *Gulliver's Travels.*

The ironic style is in evidence in his *Modest Proposal* where he puts forward the idea that the poor children of Ireland should be raised for the dining table of the rich Englishmen. The satiric motive seems to portray the poverty of the Irish people and the indifference of politicians to their plight. The proposal is expressed in quiet realistic matter-of-fact-tone of the merchant who wants to convince his customers of the quality of his articles. The distinction between animals and children is completely obliterated.

"I have been assured by a very knowing American of my acquaintance in London, that a young healthy child well nursed is at a year old a most delicious nourishing and wholesome food whether stewed, roasted, baked or boiled...always advising the mother to let them suck plentifully in the last month, so as to render them plump and fat for a good table." It is the brilliant example of Swift's irony where he suggests that children of Ireland will be taken better care, if they are bred for the table of the rich. The irony communicates indignation at the plight of children with artistic restraint. We find the full perfection of the art of irony in *Gulliver's Travels* which Swift had continued to master all through his career.

In Swift's masterpiece, *Gulliver's Travels* irony is fused with allegory. In his first voyage Gulliver finds himself in Lilliput which is peopled by six inches tall people. Their emperor who is taller just by the breadth of the nail is described as "most mighty emperor of Lilliput, delight and terror of the universe whose dominion extends five thousand blustrugs to the extremes of globe; monarch of all monarchs, taller than sons of men whose feet press down to the centre and whose head strikes against the sun." The verbal irony lies in the contrast of the size of the emperor and the high sounding majestic adjectives that form his title. It is a satire on the contemporary English king as well as the kings of all times and climes who are clothed in words and phrases of splendour while they possess the opposite qualities. The irony of situation can be discerned in the contrast between the theoretical emphasis on the moral character of the candidates and the practice of real selection of candidates and rewards on the basis of the diversions each candidate provided to please the emperor. It is a funny perception of the duality of the principle and the practice at the court of the time and all times. The physical size of the Lilliputians represent their moral and intellectual size as they indulge in their malice, conspiracy, hypocrisy and ingratitude. They are a reflection of the English people as well as mankind.

The voyage to Brobdingnag presents a contrast not only between the physical size of Lilliputians and Brobdingnagians but also their moral and spiritual size. The people in Brobdingnag are sixty foot tall and Gulliver appears like a Lilliputian or an insect by the side of a Brobdingnagian. The entire context provides the irony of situation. The Brobdingnagians are just the reverse of what the Lilliputians were. In sharp contrast with the malicious, hypocritical, ungrateful attitude of the Lilliputians, the Brobdingnagians are magnanimous. While the Lilliputians attacked Gulliver with arrows and spears at first sight, the Brobdingnagians take care of him and are amused at the toy-like man in the form of Gulliver. The devastating irony is present in the conversation between Gulliver and the king. In order to please the king, Gulliver tells him about bombs and explosive arms and ammunitions which can destroy houses and cities in no time and keep the enemy under subjugation. The king was struck with horror that an insect-like Gulliver could entertain such inhuman ideas and could be "wholly unmoved" at all by the scenes of blood and destruction which he had painted. His opinion is that some evil genius, an enemy to mankind must have contrived it. Gulliver attributes the remark of the king to his ignorance and narrow-mindedness from which the countries of Europe were excepted. The final comment of the king is that Englishmen were the most pernicious race of odious little vermin that nature ever suffered to crawl upon the surface of the earth.

The voyage to Laputa, the third voyage has an ironic framework. It is strange land men are engaged in strange scientific and philosophical speculations and experiments like extracting sunbeams out of cucumber. The professors at the school of Projectors in Lagado, the capital of Balnibarbi are working at impractical schemes. They are much more interested in hypothetical speculations than facts. As a natural corollary, the practical side of their life is clumsy and neglected. Their houses are out of shape. The irony is also found in the description of the king of Luggnagg who killed any courtier with a poison by whom he was offended. Later on he had the floor wiped out clean. But once the floor was not cleaned properly and an innocent courtier died of poison. But the king took no action against the servant whose neglect of duty caused this death. The irony also lies in Gulliver's dream of human immortality and its contrast with the plight of the Struldbrugs who are a group of immortal persons.

As the entire work of *Gulliver's Travels* presents the ironical vision, the voyage to the land of Houyhnhnms is the climax of the book. The land is populated by horses or Houyhnhnms who are perfectly reasonable and Yahoos who resemble human beings in their form and irrationality. Gulliver tells the Houyhnhnm master about the human world. They are so uncorrupt that they fail to understand how lying is possible. Gulliver's description of the profession of lawyers is also ironical. Gulliver is impressed by the irrationality of the Houyhnhnms and repulsed by the irrational behaviour of Yahoos. But the perfectly reasonable Houyhnhnms are devoid of human emotion. The irony is perceptible when, at the time, of his departure, Gulliver feels the pangs of parting and the Houyhnhnms are completely unmoved by this event. Later, Gulliver himself is the victim of Swift's irony when Gulliver trembles with fear and disgust even at the sight of his family members as he identifies them with Yahoos.

Gulliver's Travels is a satire on the English or European man as well as mankind. It is a satire on the smallness of man, vanity and illusions, his administration, politics, rivalries, malice, hypocrisy and above all, the pride of man. *Gulliver Travels* takes the form of a series of voyages and lands us in the land of Lilliput peopled by small men, Brobdingnag, peopled by giant size men, Laputa, the land of scientists and philosophers and the land of the Houyhnhnms and the Yahoos. Swift strips the human world of the film of familiarity as it is represented allegorically. Irony is the staple vehicle of Swift's satire. It is on account of irony that the datum of fiction acquires duality of vision and perception. At points, irony produces the fun of comedy and humour but mainly reveals the stark perception of the upside down view of the human outlook. The effect of irony is devastating and it completely destroys the pride of man.

12

MISANTHROPY OF SWIFT IN *GULLIVER'S TRAVELS*

Jonathan Swift's *Gulliver's Travels* is a satire on Englishmen of the eighteenth century in particular and mankind in general in the form of the book of voyages by the voyager, Lemuel Gulliver. Ever since the book was written in 1726, a bitter controversy regarding the misanthropy of Swift has raged and divided critics. The critics who consider Swift a misanthrope and those who take the opposite view of the matter present equally strong reasons in favour of their views. T.O. Wedel, J.F. Ross, R.J. Crane and Samuel H. Monk, the modern critics belong to the second set of critics who do not charge Jonathan Swift with misanthropy. The controversy moves around the question whether Gulliver can be identified with Swift or treated as an independent character in *Gulliver's Travels.*

Gulliver's Travels is not a personal satire. Jonathan Swift has created the character of Lemuel Gulliver who goes voyaging around the world to four countries, authentically recounting his experiences in all the four countries. But it is completely different from a book of voyage like Daniel Defoe's *Robinson Crusoe* because of the ironic vision of the book. Swift in his letter to Alexanders Pope dated 29th September, 1725 wrote:

"The chief end I propose to myself in all my labours is to vex the world rather than divert it. I have hated all nations, professions and communities and all my love is towards individuals: for instance, I hate the tribe of lawyers but I love counsellor such-a-one, Judge such-a-one; for so with Physician (I will not speak of my own trade), soldiers, English Scotch, French and the rest. But principally, I hate and detest that animal called man, although I heartily love John, Peter, Thomas and so forth.... I have got materials towards a treatise, proving the falsity of that definition *animal rationale* to show it should be only *rationis capax*. Upon this great foundation of misanthropy (Though not Timon's manners) the whole building of my *Travels* is erected...." The other letter of Swift records the following: "I tell you after all that I do not hate mankind; it is *vous autres* who hate them because you would have them reasonable animals and are angry for being disappointed." The spirit of the two letters is the same. In the second letter, Swift states that man is not a rational animal but capable of reason. Those who consider him reasonable animal hate him because they are angry and disappointed. Swift only reflects over the deficiency of man ironically.

Gulliver, the central point of misanthropy controversy, is just the looking glass for Swift. A semblance of fictional reality has been imparted to him. *Gulliver's Travels* is a second person's account. The lense of Swift diminifies in Lilliput, magnifies in Brobdingnag, scrutinises philosophic and scientific activity in Laputa and magnifies the beastly and rational aspects of man in the land of Houyhnhnms yet the question stares in the face whether Gulliver has a separate identity or is Swift himself.

Gulliver's voyage to Lilliput where the people are not more than six inches tall represent the European and English men and their system in terms of their smallness in ethical and moral aspects—their malice, flattery, ingratitude and hypocrisy and meanness of ambition. The Prince of Brobdingnag, after getting an account of the Englishmen through Gulliver, comments that they are "the most pernicious race of odious little vermin that nature ever suffered to crawl upon the surface of the earth." The voyage to Laputa is a satire on the useless speculations and experiments in which scientists and philosophers are engaged. It is only when we reach the land of Houyhnhnms that we are faced with the problem of misanthropy of Gulliver or Swift in the book.

Swift presents Houyhnhnms and Yahoos not as his symbols of man because Gulliver himself is the symbol of humanity who shares somehow the nature of both the extremes. Swift simply isolates the two elements that combine in the duality of man, the middle link to allow Gulliver to contemplate each in its essence. Gulliver is dazzled by the Houyhnhnms, the embodiment of pure reason, the creatures of rationalistic utopia. They know neither love nor grief nor ambition. They harbour natural human affection for each other but they love everyone equally. It is said that the Houyhnhnms stand for Swift's ideal man but the Houyhnhnms are Cartesian, while Swift is anti-Cartesian. Swift's first published satire "Thoughts on Various Subjects" exhibits his anti-Cartesianism as he says, "The social scheme of supplying our wants, by lopping off our feet while we want shoes." George Orwell's remarks on the Houyhnhnms only applies this comment of Swift to the Houyhnhnms: "They (Houyhnhnms) are exempt from love, friendship, curiosity, fear, sorrow and except in their feeling towards the Yahoos who occupy rather the same place in their community as the Jews in Nazi Germany—anger and hatred. The Houyhnhnms, creatures without history continue generation after generation to live prudently, maintaining their population exactly at the same level avoiding all passions, suffering from no diseases, meeting death indifferently, training up their young in the same principles—and all for what? In order that the same process may continue indefinitely."

We seem to recognize Swift's voice, powerful and compelling and sounding with genius in the intensity with which Gulliver feels repulsion against the Yahoos, the symbol of the degenerate man who does not use his capacity to lead the life of reason. The Houyhnhnms regarded the British institutions as "the result of gross defect in reason and by consequence in virtue. Gulliver's disgust for the human species increases steadily as the narrative proceeds and Gulliver learns to live as the humble admirer and servant of the Houyhnhnms.

We feel like agreeing with Samuel H. Monk when he remarks, "The meaning of the book is wholly distorted if we identify the Gulliver of the last voyage with his creator and lay Gulliver's misanthropy at Swift's door. Gulliver is a fully objective and dramatic character, no more to be identified with Swift than Shylock is to be identified with Shakespeare." Monk's point is further developed by John F. Ross in his essay, "The Final Comedy of Lemuel Gulliver." He divides the satire of *Gulliver's Travels* into the corrosive satire and the comic satire. According to Ross "Swift, the satirist and realist is well aware that there is more of the Yahoo in humanity than there is benevolence and reason. He develops his attack by means of corrosive satire in terms of pessimism and misanthropy. He knows there is much to be hated in the animal called man, but he knows there are individuals he loves." Swift's comic satire develops where Swift can differentiate between Yahoo and Gulliver but Gulliver is convinced that he is a Yahoo. Gulliver is convinced that human beings are worse than the Yahoos and tries to transform himself into a horse by trying to trot like a horse and converse with it. The insufficiency of Gulliver's attitude comes to light when he continues to "tremble between fear and hatred" at the sight of men. By his own account, he comes into contact with honest, kindly and generous human beings but he is so much obsessed with his rigid, biased and oversimplified attitude that he cannot believe the evidence of his own experience. The severe satire remains the same but at the same time Swift comments on the insufficiency of the corrosive attitude. The evil in the world and man may drive to pessimism and misanthropy. Nevertheless Swift demonstrates such an attitude to be inadequate. "Swift is laughing at Gulliver, a part of himself not with Gulliver but above him" as Gulliver can see only the Yahoo in man. Swift is not disgusted with mankind as Gulliver is as he shows the absurdity of such a point of view through the consequent and subsequent behaviour of Gulliver. It is better to settle this controversy with Swift's own words in "Verse on the Death of Dr. Swift:"

> Perhaps I may allow the Dean
> Had too much satire in his vein
> And seemed determined not to starve it
> Because no age could more deserve it.
> Yet malice never was his aim.

13

Swift as a Misogynist in *Gulliver's Travels*

Swift is considered a misanthrope and also a misogynist. Such assumptions are based on a few facts of Swift's life as well as by confusing the identity of Gulliver with Swift. We shall have to examine carefully the evidence put forward in support of the assumption of Swift as a misogynist.

Some critics find a strange contradiction in Swift's relation with women. Throughout his life he felt the need of the female company. He sincerely loved Stella and was loved by her. Stella was actually Esther Johnson, a beautiful young woman, the illegitimate daughter of William Temple who loved Swift ever since they met in the house of Temple. The letters written to Esther Johnson were collected under the title *The Journal to Stella.* The death of Esther Johnson dealt a heavy blow to him but he silently bore the death of one of the best loved person in his life. The relation of Jonathan Swift to Esther Johnson is not a tale of unrequited love. It is another matter that for some unknown reason they could not marry. Those who consider Jonathan Swift as a misogynist cite the relationship of Jonathan Swift with a lady whom he called Venessa. She was actually Hester Vanhomrigh who loved him passionately and he also loved her. When she wanted to establish closer intimacy with him, he broke her heart by his extreme cruelty. Those who find a contradiction in Swift's attitude to women blame Swift for not marrying her. They also say that he had a strong desire to have the company of women and to enjoy their witty conversation. But this intimacy created sexual desire in women. But he was disgusted with the animal desire of women. A woman with such desires appeared to him to be the agent of the devil in the world to tempt man. They say that Swift did not believe in married love or married happiness. How far such an analysis of Swift's life is correct is difficult to say but the evidence that they bring from *Gulliver's Travels* does not point in the same direction.

Some critics have noted that in *Gulliver's Travels* women whom Gulliver meets in the various lands are either whimsical or vicious. In Lilliput he saved the Queen's palace from fire by urinating on it. The Queen however instead of being grateful to him became his enemy. But this portrayal of the Queen is based on the character of Queen Anne who harboured a prejudice against Swift for writing a book, *The Tale of Tub* and never considered him fit for the post of the bishop. So from this portrayal, it cannot be inferred that Swift paints the female character in unfavourable light. We cannot deny that the portrayal of the wife of the Prime Minister in Laputa is not favourable. He treats her life well. But she came down to Lagado and was found with a drunkard who beat her everyday. The husband did not reproach her and treated her with kindness. She managed to steal down again to her lover in Lagado. The maids of honour in the Queen's Court in Laputa were coquettish and passionate creatures. Gulliver says, "They would often strip me naked from top to toe and lay me at full length on their bosoms. The handsomest among them, a pleasant frolicsome girl of sixteen would sometime set me astride upon one of her nipples with many other tricks wherein the reader will excuse me for not being over particular."

It may be pointed out that if Swift presents many faceted realities of life or the woman, it is not his misogyny. The passion in girls is as natural as in a boy. Swift's portrayal of the tender, lovable and reasonable Glumdalclitch is probably modelled on Stella or Esther Johnson. It is also pointed out that in Brobdingnag Gulliver is not attracted to the naked bodies of the girls in the Queen's apartments and they appeared to him loathsome. He is also shocked at the sight of the breasts and nipples of abnormal size. When the disgust towards the female body is noted the fact is neglected that the disproportionate size of the breast and the nipple accounts for the disgust. Gulliver also points out that they appear quite attractive to the males of their size just as the English ladies appear to their lovers. So this evidence of misogyny from *Gulliver's Travels* is unacceptable.

Gulliver's experience of horror in the Houyhnhnmland when he bathes naked in the pond and a naked female Yahoo jumps into the water and embraces him passionately has been cited as a case of misogyny. But it should be also noted that Gulliver belongs to a species different from the Yahoos, though they are similar to man in the human form. At the last, the horror comes also from the difference of species. We can only say on the basis of the study of *Gulliver's Travels* that Swift cannot be charged with misogyny as with misanthropy. His portrayal of the different kinds of women and girls in *Gulliver's Travels* is based partly on reality. If realities are complex and contrary, for their portrayal Swift cannot he charged with misogyny.

14

SWIFT AS A SATIRIST IN *GULLIVER'S TRAVELS*

Jonathan Swift belonged to the eighteenth century, the age of satire. This age produced Dryden and Samuel Johnson in poetry, Goldsmith and Sheridan in drama and Jonathan Swift in prose. Dryden, Pope, Sheridan and Goldsmith took up individuals or aspects of the contemporary society for satire in their work, while Swift stands apart from the satirists of the age as he took up the whole mankind as the subject of his satire. The shadows of the contemporary world are there but he transmuted the temporal into the timeless, the local and particular into the general and universal. It is the secret of the enduring appeal of *Gulliver's Travels* from age to age in spite of the fact that the controversy about Swift's misanthropy has not died down.

However great, timeless and universal themes a writer may take up, he cannot escape the penumbra of his times and place. The England and Europe of the eighteenth century are very much present in *Gulliver's Travels.* The references to contemporary events and personalities can be easily cited in the events and figures of Lilliput, Laputa and Houyhnhnmland. The land of Lilliput presents the picture of contemporary England. The two struggling political parties in Lilliput which are distinguished by the high-heeled shoes and the low-heeled shoes are the two English political parties, the Tories and the Whigs and the inimical island of Blefuscu which poses a danger is France with which England was engaged in a long battle of supremacy. The emperor of Lilliput is George I of England. The satirical references to the mercy of the emperor is a reference to the executions which took place after the rebellion of 1715 and the praise of George I's mercy as published by the government. The scientific experiments and speculations in which the professors in Laputa are engaged is a satire on the contemporary science and the Royal Society established in 1662. The Houyhnhnms stand for the rational utopia in which the Deists and the Plegians believed. The ideas of Hobbes, Lock and Descartes are represented by these rationally perfect images of Houyhnhnms. But the greatness of Swift lies in transmuting the temporal society into something rich and strange, timeless and universal.

Swift adopts the fictional method of the voyage literature of his time. Like Daniel Defoe in *Robinson Crusoe* he creates a fictional character in the form of Gulliver who appears to present the realistic account of his voyages. His visits to Lilliput, Brobdingnag, Laputa and Houyhnhnmland are nothing but striping the contemporary world of the film of familiarity and presenting the human world in strange colours of fantasy, making the familiar strange and strange familiar and revealing ironically the evils of the familiar world. Thus his satire takes the form in which satire in fused with allegory.

Irony is the staple vehicle of Swift in *Gulliver's Travels* and other works of Swift. There is verbal irony as well as the irony of situation. Here is the description of the emperor of Lilliput who is a little more than six inches tall as he is taller than others just by the breadth of the nail:

> Golbasto Momaren Evlame Gurdito Shefin Mrsully most mighty emperor of Lilliput, delight and terror of the universe, whose dominions extend five thousand blustrugs (about twelve miles in circumference) to the extremities of the globe, monarch of all monarchs, taller than sons of men; whose feet press down to the centre and whose head strikes against the sun; at where nod the princes of the earth shake their knees, pleasant as the spring, comfortable as the summer, fruitful as autumn, dreadful as winter...." (chap iii. Book I)

The satiric force depends on our knowledge of his size. His pride is absurd when we compare his pigmy physique with the elaborate honourable title he attached to his personality. The irony only brings the discrepancy to the recognition of daylight. It generates no bitterness but the pure fun as in a mock heroic poem like *The Rape of the Lock.* The same technique is reversed in Book II in Brobdingnag where Gulliver appears like a pigmy beside the sixty-foot tall Brobdingnagians. There is reliance on direct, sensory physical effects. The power of surface simplicity derives from the symbolism beneath. The first Brobdingnagian examines Gulliver as small dangerous animal that may scratch or bite such as "weasel." Gulliver himself fears he may be dashed to the ground as "any hateful, little animal" a man has a mind to destroy. The size is only relative and has a relative symbolic significance. Their size reflects their broad heart and mind in contrast with the heart and mind of the Lilliputians. The contrast of the speculative project, of the Laputans with their actual realization is at the root of the irony in the third book as the contrast between the rational horses (Houyhnhnms) and the irrational men-like creatures (Yahoos) and Gulliver's identification of man with the Yahoo and his desire to turn into one of such horses create all the ironic drama in the fourth book of *Gulliver's Travels.* The irony turns savage though quite amusing and interesting when Gulliver attributes direct criticism of man by the Brobdingnagian king to his ignorance and narrow-minded prejudice, for example, his consideration of men as the most pernicious race of little odious virmin that nature ever suffered to crawl upon the surface of the earth.

The satire of Swift is imaginative and creative in the sense that he gives to airy nothing a local habitation and a name and seems to present a realistic account of the worlds really visited by Gulliver during his four voyages. The datum of his realistic fiction is utraquistic. The innocent account of the strange lands and people has been so carefully presented that it reflects in its symbolic details of the miniature world the reality of familiar human world and also its contrasts with it. This is why it can serve as the "Children's classics" as well as a satire on the pride of the degenerate man.

The satire of Swift is concerned with the contemporary world as the satires of Dryden. But Swift is able to transmute the temporal into the timeless, the particular into the universal like all great art. It is also notable that the irony of Swift is not only savage and bitter but comic and funny and even at the cost of Gulliver. The narrator was upto the nineteenth century identified with his creator. *Gulliver's Travels* is certainly rich and complex in its texture and structure. This is why every age reads a different meaning in the book and the controversy about the meaning of the book goes on. The satirical treatment of man in the hands of Swift has an intellectual depth unprecedented in English literature. He differs from Pope in his view of man where the situation of man is not "the isthmus of a middle state" but pride is associated with the degenerate man. Swift's *Gulliver's Travels* vexes the world with its "misanthropy" as it explodes the vanity and pride of man by holding up a mirror which reflects the truth of man.

15

The Prose Style of Swift in *Gulliver's Travels*

Herbert Read remarks in *English Prose Style* about Jonathan Swift's prose style: "However widely his vision might extend, however deep his insight, his mode of expressions remained simple and single and clearly comprehensible." Swift himself draws attention to simplicity as a virtue, for example, in a "Letter to a young Gentleman" where he refers to "simplicity, without which no human performance can arrive to any great perfection." Such remarks of Swift on prose style divert critics' attention from the real secret of Swift's greatness as a prose writer to the plain surface simplicity of his plain prose. The description of Gulliver's arrival on the shore of Lilliput and the early pages of each of the four books where a brief account is given of the commonplace circumstances leading to his adventure into a brave new world are the finest illustrations of Swift's dry, simple, plain matter-of-fact style. Swift, here, adopts the narrative style of contemporary books of travels but "the mode of expression" is not simple and single and not clearly comprehensible in the rest of the narrative. That would be to separate his prose from his peculiarly ironic motive which drives the green fuse between the simple plain surface and the metaphorical (allegorical) apprehension of his vision.

It is generally supposed that Swift was the typical product of the eighteenth century scientific temper which was reflected in his simple rational and ordered prose style. Swift's prose style does not reflect the new intellectual virtues as it is not the style of one who followed what Basil Willey refers to as the plain path of "Nature and Reason." He belongs to the tradition of Rabelais, Donne and Ben Jonson in his brilliant play with old mode of learned speculation, his imaginative fertility in developing concretely a pseudo-scientific conception, his dialectical resourcefulness and effrontery. The Augustan economy of Swift's prose cannot be studied in isolation. The plainness and simplicity do not define the essence and nature of Swift's greatness. Swift modifies the dialectic method of speculative philosophy of the earlier periods to achieve his aims which in turn modify his own style.

In his earlier work, *A Tale of a Tub* (1704) Swift displays his ability to play with learned ideas and create a comic conception. His model was the French writer, Rabelais who was translated into English during 1670's not long before Swift started writing his satires. In the third book of Rabelais, a character, Panurge who runs through his three years' income in a fortnight borrows ideas for astronomy, physiology and other branches of knowledge to prove that borrowing and lending is the very principle on which the whole universe runs. The witty application of learned ideas in support of an audacious conclusion is discernible in the Metaphysical poets which involves a parody of the pre-scientific methods of speculation and was discredited by the new scientists. Though this is the typical style of Swift, it can be seen in Lawrence Sterne's *Tristram Shandy* as well.

The Metaphysical way of arguing through images for the first time appears in his early book, *The Battle of Books* (1704) in which the spider who tries to score his superiority over the bee ends up by producing the opposite effects:

> Your livelihood is a universal plunder on Nature; a freebooter over Fields and Gardens, and for the sake of stealing, will rob a nettle as readily as a violet whereas I am a domestick animal furnisht with a native stock within myself. The large castle is all built with my own hands and materials extracted altogether out of my own person.

The quarrel between the spider and the bee symbolically represents the dispute between the ancient and the modern writers.

The later work of Swift needed a straight-forward factual treatment but the concrete details are charged with a peculiar intensity and are used to give "an unexpected force and nuance to an argument." Though the learned ideas are dropped but the arts of argument have been intensified. The wit of such techniques is of the previous age when dialectic or the ability to dispute on both sides was part of the education. But this dialectical dexterity of Donne, Dryden and Swift declined after the new philosophers and scientists appeared on the scene. In his *Modest Proposal* like *Gulliver's Travels* Swift cultivated his art of the statement of double entendre. In *Modest Proposal, The Drapier's Letters* and *Gulliver's Travels,* there is the creation of a fictitious character and the language appropriate to the character is quite artistically manipulated where he exhibits his power of destructive juxtaposition of words and phrases pregnant with irony. Not only in his early works images abound but the device of arguing through images is present in *Gulliver's Travels.* The Yahoo is the image of man from whom reason is withheld and the Houyhnhnms are the impossible and unhuman standard of rational perfection. Their history does not contain the event of the Fall. They do not know the dignity and glory of man. They are completely undisturbed by the irrational impulses. Gulliver stands between the Yahoo and the Houyhnhnm but identifies man with the Yahoo. The terrible satirical force in the fourth book of *Gulliver's Travels* derives from Gulliver's conversion to the standpoint of the Houyhnhnms. It is the device of the fictional character which helps him describe the object of satire from the satirical point of view. Gulliver uses apparently innocuous statements in the description of the human wickedness, lie, greed and the profession of the lawyer etc. to the unsympathetic, rationally perfect audience of the Houyhnhnms who are uncontaminated by such evils. The apparent detachment of Gulliver in the description of the human world seems innocuous but it is deliberately devised to achieve the devastating and comic effect of the writing.

Jonathan Swift's prose is apparently simple, plain and matter-of-fact in style. But it is only the deceptive surface. It does not reflect the eighteenth century scientific temper. On the other hand, the simple matter-of-fact surface conceals beneath it the fertility of the writer's imagination. It abounds in images and the mode of apprehension is metaphorical.

These images derive their great satirical and comic force from the situation which is dressed in the subtle irony which is at the service of Swift, the satirist. Swift does not belong to the tradition of Addison and Steele but extends the dialectical art of Rabelais, Donne and Dryden.

16

The Portrayal of the Eighteenth Century Life

Gulliver's Travels by Jonathan Swift is a great satire on mankind. Very few eighteenth century satires possess the depths and intensity of *Gulliver's Travels.* There is great imaginative and creative fertility which gives to airy nothing a local habitation and a name. Lilliput, Brobdingnag, Laputa and Houyhnhnmland do not stand on the map of the world. But they acquire a palpable reality through the creative imagination of Swift.

However great a work of art may be, it cannot escape the penumbra of its time and place. Thus Swift has also transmuted the particular into the general and the temporal into the timeless and universal in *Gulliver's Travels.* The allegorical and symbolic details of Lilliput, Brobdingnag, Laputa and Houyhnhnmland represent the English and European life in the time of Swift or the eighteenth century, only the light thrown on the eighteenth century life is satirical.

The first voyage of Gulliver lands him in Lilliput where the people are six inches high and their houses, trees and animals are accordingly small. They are like toys and dolls to Gulliver. Lilliput reflects on the smallness of means, the vanity of motives, the illusion of catchwords through which the kings retain their thrones and magistrate their office and the fearful influence of man upon man is exercised. The spirit of the age is reflected in the sycophancy and flattery in the courts through the metaphor of aspirants of high ranks and ministers dancing to the rhythm of the stick in the hand of the king. The red, blue and green ribbons by which the courtiers are rewarded represent the awards instituted by Queen Anne in 1703, by

George I in 1725 and the one bestowed upon Walpole in 1726 respectively.

The conflict between Big-Endians and Small-Endians represents the religious wars between the Catholic France and the Protestant England. The conflict between the High-Heeled and the Low-Heeled parties represents the Whig and the Tory, the two political parties in England and their quarrels. Blefuscu stands for France and Lilliput for England and the war between the two is the real war between these two countries.

The empress who harbours a prejudice against Gulliver after extinguishing fire in her apartment by urinating on it is actually Queen Anne who after the publication of *A Tale of Tub* was suspicious of Swift and never considered him fit for the position of a bishop and he had to remain content with the position of the dean at St. Patrick's in Dublin. Bolgolam represents the Earl of Nottingham who used his influence to block Swift's promotion. Flimnap, the Lord Treasurer of Lilliput is Sir Robert Walpole who displayed his skill in the art of parliamentary and political intrigues. There is also a close parallel between Gulliver and Lord Bolingbroke. Like Gulliver, he brought a great war to an end between England and France. Like Gulliver, he was condemned by his political opponents for not bringing about the complete surrender of the enemy and was accused of culpable association with French ambassadors. Thus the contemporary England of the time of Swift is transmuted into the symbolic details of the allegory.

Swift transposes the scale in Lamuel Gulliver's voyage to Brobdingnag. While in Lilliput Gulliver was among the dolls in Brobdingnag where people are sixty-foot high, Gulliver is himself like a doll among the giants. The former was the parody of the human reality which custom invests with grandeur, in the latter, the human reality reveals itself as ridiculous and infinitely small. There is not a close parallel between England and Brobdingnag. The Gulliver's account of the English and the European life before the king of Brobdingnag brings to our mind the institution of England, both political, social and otherwise.

The third voyage of Gulliver brings him to Laputa and its Academy of Lagado. It is a satire on the Royal Society established in England in 1662 as well as a comment on man's relation to nature and the relation between England and Ireland. According to Marjorie Nicolson and Nora Mohler all the Projects in the Academy of Lagado in which Projectors or Professors are engaged is based on the *Philosophical Transactions* of the Royal Society. The entire chapter is directed against the impractical and useless scientific experiments like extracting sunrays from cucumber. Swift here represents his own and the general scepticism about the experiments and the discoveries of science.

The way the king of Laputa, the flying island, lowers the island, throws stones at the rebellious below on the continent reflects the way England oppresses and suppresses the people and their rebellion in Ireland. Swift does not trust the scientific knowledge of Bentley and Newton's Theory of gravitation. Swift in this voyage sums up the general attitude about the uselessness of scientific inquiry when he applauds the Brobdingnagians because their study of mathematics is wholly applied what may be useful in life to the improvement of Agriculture and all Mechanical Arts. In the same vein, the king of Brobdingnag dismisses all the race of politicians of England and Europe and claims that those who increase the agricultural output are far better than all the race of politicians together.

In the voyage to the country of the Houyhnhnms Swift's satire rises to an intensity where Swift's intention is "to vex the world" by writing *Gulliver's Travels.* The world of the Houyhnhnms is placed in sharp contrast to the English and European society and their institutions. The noble horses, the Houyhnhnms are presented as the symbol of the rational perfection and the Yahoos, human in form and figure, whom they rule over, are filthy, unreasonable and full of corruption. They are identified with the English and European man. The Houyhnhnms are completely uncontaminated by evil and corruption so much so that Gulliver has to define evils of the European life like lying, the profession of the lawyers and judges in order to explain to them. The Houyhnhnm master is unable to understand them. Their language has no word for the kind of evils associated with the English or European society. Houyhnhnms are considered ideal by Gulliver and words like power, government, war, law, punishment and lie are beyond the comprehension of Houyhnhnms but they are part of the English or European society. The king of Brobdingnag understands Gulliver's account of the English life and institutions and points out the possibilities of corruption in such institutions. But to the rationally ideal creatures, they are completely incomprehensible. Thus the English or European man is fully identified with the irrational Yahoos. The European life and institutions do not compare well with the Houyhnhnms and do not find favour with them.

Jonathan Swift has creatively but satirically used the details of the contemporary English and European life. They have been transmuted into the allegorical symbols and acquire the timeless and universal significance. The creative process by which they are alchemised into a work of art accounts for the greatness of Swift's artistic imagination and satiric force which even his detractors recognise as "the product of extraordinary genius."

QUESTIONS OF ANSWERS

(i) Show that Gulliver's Travels is more than an Adventure Story.

Or

"Gulliver's Travels is a children's Classics." Comment.

Answer *See* G.T. As a Children's classics on page 102.

(ii) Examine the structure of *Gulliver's Travels.*

Answer *See* the Structure of G.T. on page 106.

(iii) Bring out Swift's satirical Technique in G.T.

Or

Comment on the Irony in G.T.

Answer *See* Irony in G.T. on page 110.

(iv) G.T. is a great satiric masterpiece. Discuss.

Or

Comment on Swift as a Satirist in G.T.

Answer *See* Swift as a Satirist on page 122.

(v) Consider Swift as a Misanthrope in G.T.

Or

Does Swift hate mankind? Elaborate your answer with complete evidence from G.T.

Answer *See* Misanthropy of Swift on page 115.

(vi) Discuss the Prose Style of Swift in G.T.

Answer *See* the Prose Style of Swift on page 126.

(vii) Consider Swift as a Misogynist in G.T.

Answer *See* Swift as a Misogynist on page 119.

(viii) Swift transmutes the topical and the temporal into something timeless and universal in G.T. Discuss.

Answer *See* the significance of four voyages on page 94.

(ix) Swift captures the spirit of the Age in his great satiric masterpiece. Explain.

Answer *See* the Portrayal of the Eighteenth Century Life on page 130.

Bibliography

(i) *Swift: An Introduction* By Ricardo Quintana

(ii) *Swift* Ed. By Ernest Toreson

(iii) *Gulliverness Travels* Ed. By Frank Brady

(iv) *The Common Pursuit* By F.R. Leavis

(v) *The Pelican Guide from Dryden to Johnson.* Ed. Boris Ford

(vi) *A History of English Literature* By Legouis & Cazamian

(vii) *A Critical History of English Literature* By David Daiches

(viii) *A History of English Literature* By J. Long